WHAT DO I WHEN TEENAGERS STRUGGLE WITH EATING DISORDERS?

Dr. Steven Gerali

youth
specialties

ZONDERVAN.com/
AUTHORTRACKER
follow your favorite authors

Contents

What Do I Do When...
BOOK SERIES
| INTRODUCTION |
Read This First!

It's very important you read this Introduction. This series of books has grown out of years of listening to professional and volunteer youth workers wrestle through difficult ministry situations. I usually know what's coming when the conversation starts with, "What do I do when...?" Most of the time they're looking for remedial help, but many times the issues covered in this book series have no preventive measures available. Many of these issues aren't given serious thought until they evidence themselves in the fabric of ministry. Then youth workers, church staff, parents, and even teenagers scramble to get some kind of understanding, remedy, support, or theological perspective on the situation. This series is designed to help you.

Before we move too far ahead, you need to know a few things. First, just because you read these books and acquire some helping skills, that doesn't make you a professional counselor or caregiver. In many situations you'll need to help parents and teenagers network with professional mental health workers, medical professionals, or, in some cases, legal counsel. Oftentimes the quality of care regarding these issues lies in the rapid response of helping professionals. So if you don't get anything else out of this series, get this:

The best thing you can do as an effective helper is realize you're not a trained counselor and you must refer, refer, refer.

Second, often when youth workers are in the throes of an issue, they'll quickly access the Internet for help and information. Researching something online can be very time-consuming, and it can provide unreliable information. So this book series is designed to offer reliable information that's quickly accessible for anyone who's working with adolescents.

Third, each book follows a similar format designed to help you navigate the information more easily. But more importantly, it also provides a model to help you deal with the issue at hand. What Do I Do When... books are divided into the following four sections:

SECTION 1: UNDERSTANDING THE ISSUE, OR "PRESENTING PROBLEM"

Each book will start with an *epistemology* of the issue—in other words, the knowledge regarding its nature and scope. Many youth workers formulate their opinions, beliefs, and ideas using faulty information that's been passed through the grapevine—often without realizing the grapevine has root rot. Faulty information can change the trajectory of our actions in such a way it actually causes us to miss the mark. And many times our "misses" can be destructive to a kid who's already struggling with a painful issue.

We cannot expect to lead a teenager to the truth of Scripture if we start with a foundation that's built upon a lie or deception. We must be informed, seeking to understand the presenting problem as learners with a teachable spirit. In some cases these books may provide only the basics about an issue. But hopefully they'll be enough to create a solid foundation that gives direction for further research from reliable sources.

SECTION 2: UNDERSTANDING HOW YOUR THEOLOGY INTERSECTS THE ISSUE OR PRESENTING PROBLEM

Each book will also cover at least one theological perspective that informs the situation. However, please note I plan to give theological insights from multiple perspectives, so you'll know the theological voices adolescents and their families hear. Some of these voices may not resonate with your particular view, but it's important you develop a gracious, loving, and understanding heart. Keep in mind you're dealing with desperate, hurting, and broken people who—in the midst of their pain and struggle—are seeking grace and hope, not someone with theological answers.

I realize there's a danger in writing like this. Whenever the playing field is leveled—in other words, when one's internalized theological framework is challenged or an opposing theological view is given—it can quickly become a fisticuffs arena to champion truth. I believe that truth brings freedom (John 8:32). But let's remember that the Pharisees believed they'd cornered the market on truth simply because they held to a rigid interpretation of the Scriptures, yet they failed to listen for God's voice in others—especially in the Messiah.

A dear friend of mine once confronted a group of students by asking, "Is your interpretation of Scripture always right?" The students knew that if they replied affirmatively, then they'd set themselves up as the source of infallibility. So they replied, "No, nobody can be right all the time."

My friend then asked, "In what areas are you wrong?"

His wisdom during that loving confrontation helped those students see that unless they openly and graciously engaged the theological perspectives of others, they'd never know if their own perspectives were lacking. Our goal in helping kids through difficult issues is to usher Christ into their situations. Many times that may not be with answers but with presence, affection, support, and understanding.

I recall a situation in which my dear, sweet, Italian mother was hurting for a young couple who'd been caught in sexual sin (she and my dad had mentored this couple). The disciplinary actions of the church were harsh and shaming. So while the church acted in rightness, it failed to see other theological perspectives that informed this situation, such as a theology of reconciliation, grace, confession, and absolution. In my conversation with my mother, I heard her engage these things because she, too, entered into the process and pain of this young couple, and she refused to apply a static template of dealing with the issue in a "right way." Instead, she decided to deal with the issue first in a loving and good way.

It's important to remember that many times rightness is not goodness. God has called his people to be good (Matthew 5:16, Ephesians 2:10, 1 Timothy 6:17-19)—not always "right." That doesn't mean we ignore truth, nor does it mean we minimize the authority of Scripture. It just means we must be incredibly and painfully careful to err on the side of that which is loving and good. Wrestling through various theological viewpoints, even if we don't initially agree with them, will keep us in the tension of being loving and good.

SECTION 3: CONSIDERING WHAT ACTIONS WE CAN TAKE

When we understand an issue or problem, we must wrestle through the theological and consider appropriate action. That can mean anything from doing more research to aggressively seeking solutions. In this third section, I'll attempt to provide you with a framework for action, including practical examples, applications, and tips. This will only be a skeletal plan you'll need to own and tweak to fit the uniqueness of your situation. There is rarely one prescribed action for an issue—every situation is unique because of the people involved.

Throughout the years, I've watched youth workers attempt to use books about youth ministry as one uses an instruction manual for the assembly of a bicycle. They assume that if they put this screw into this hole, then this part will operate correctly. Likewise, they expect that applying a tip from a book will fix a student or situation. If only life were this easy!

Every example provided in this series of books grows out of my years of ministry and clinical experience, input from God's people, and proven results. But they're not foolproof solutions. God desires to be intimately involved in the lives of students and their families, as they trust in God through their difficult times. There is no fix-all formula—just faithfulness. So as you follow some of the directives or action steps in these books, remember you must prayerfully seek God in the resolution of the issues.

SECTION 4: ADDITIONAL RESOURCES

In this section I'll provide some reliable resources for further help. These Internet sites, books, and organizations can assist you in mobilizing help for teenagers and their families. Hopefully this will save you many hours of hunting, so you can better invest in your students and their families.

Where needed, I'll also give a brief comment or description for the source. For example, some sources will serve to explain a different theological perspective from mainstream. This will help you to be informed before you run out and buy the book or engage the Web site.

I trust this book series will assist you in the critical care of teenagers and their families. God has put you on the front lines of attending, shepherding, and training people who are very dear and valuable to his heart. The way you respond to each person who's involved in these critical issues may have eternal consequences. My prayer is that everyone who reads these books will be empowered in a new way to usher Jesus more deeply and practically into the lives of precious teenagers.

Understanding Eating Disorders

| Section 1 |

Anna, a high school junior, is active, trustworthy, and seemingly stable. Her youth pastor, Sue, calls Anna a "core student" because she makes friends easily and is very relationally engaging. Anna appears to be a normal teenage girl.

Sue began to suspect something wasn't right with Anna during summer camp. Anna came to the cafeteria for every meal, but she wouldn't eat anything. When confronted, Anna said she didn't like the camp's food. While this was true of many students, they still managed to make meals out of salads, cereal, and peanut butter and jelly. However, Anna's case seemed different. She never evidenced that "famished" look that a typical teen has even when they don't like the food. Occasionally, Anna would nibble at something like a bowl of cereal, a piece of fruit, or a slice of bread—but Sue began to believe this was just a smoke screen to throw everybody off.

Anna and her friends often talked about diets and how fat they looked, and Sue always reassured them that they looked great. But Anna joked or dropped comments about her weight more often than the other girls did.

Sue also noticed that Anna consistently walked into the all-camp meeting times late and alone. This made Sue suspicious enough to act on her gut feelings. So one evening Sue walked to Anna's cabin after the meeting had begun. When she walked in, she noticed that Anna's suitcase was open and full of junk food. She also heard Anna throwing up in the bathroom. Sue sat on the bed and waited until Anna came out of the bathroom. Anna was caught off guard to see Sue sitting there.

"What's going on here?" Sue asked, pointing to the open suitcase.

"I hate the food here, so I brought my own," Anna replied.

"But you're throwing it all up," Sue said.

"I don't feel good," Anna said.

"I believe there's more going on here than you're admitting to," Sue said.

That opened the door for Anna to talk to Sue, and she finally admitted that she'd been bingeing and throwing up for two years.

Sue knew some of the facts and statistics surrounding eating disorders, but now the issue had become a stark reality. This condition was affecting a teen whom Sue deeply cared about—and the teen's family, too. This prompted her to call me and ask, "What do I do when a teenager struggles with an eating disorder?"

1.1 SCOPE OF THIS ISSUE

Many youth workers have a very narrow, oversimplified view of eating disorders. The belief is that teens with eating disorders simply don't eat. And if they do eat, they binge and then throw it up. Further, they believe these disorders stem from low self-esteem and vanity as teenage girls attempt to fit into a culturally conformed, media-driven ideal of beauty. While most youth workers are sympathetic to the plight of a teen struggling with this type of disorder, they may also believe the cure is to "just eat" or to relearn to eat right.

Other youth workers may take an alarmist approach believing that every teen who's on a diet or naturally skinny has an eating disorder. Overall, the majority of youth workers today understand that eating disorders are a critical issue among teenagers, yet they tend to be unaware of its presence in their own groups.

Adolescents are the primary victims of eating disorders. In spite of the efforts of national task forces to educate schoolchildren about the dangers, eating disorders are still on the rise. A teenager's need to be loved and accepted is so great that she'll literally starve herself if she believes it will accomplish that purpose. *The Wall Street Journal* reported that between 2000 and 2006, the percentage of girls who believe they must be thin to be popular rose from 48 percent to 60 percent.[1] Of those being treated with eating disorders, 86 percent reported its onset by age 20; 10 percent by age 10; 33 percent between ages 11 and 15; and 43 percent between ages 16 and 20.[2] Of the estimated 8 million Americans (1 million of which are male) who are afflicted with eating disorders, 95 percent are adolescents between the ages of 12 and 25.[3] And millions more struggle with binge eating.[4]

Anorexia nervosa is believed to be the third most chronic illness affecting teenagers today.[5] It also has the highest mortality rate of any psychiatric disorders. Its fatality rate is 12 times higher than all other causes of death to adolescent girls ages 12 to 25.[6] And most victims die from physiological complications.[7]

Obesity is another diagnosed eating disorder that is becoming common with teenagers. The Center for Disease Control has reported that between 1980 and 2000, the number of obese children and adolescents in the United States tripled. Additionally, between 2003 and 2006, the prevalence for obesity among adolescents ages 12 to 19 increased from 5 percent to 17.6 percent.[8] The sad part is that only one in ten teenagers with any of these eating disorders gets the professional treatment they require.[9]

Eating disorders aren't unique to American teenagers, but they've become a global concern. Statistics indicate that Western and Latin cultures numbers of people with eating disorders are equivocal to those of the United States. Eating disorders are a global adolescent problem that should be a concern of all youth workers.

An eating disorder is characterized by severe, abnormal disturbances in eating behaviors (ranging from not eating to eating too much to eating in an unhealthy manner) along with anxiety and preoccupation with one's body image, shape, and weight. Many times this phenomenon has a comorbidity with severe mental and physical health issues, including multiple forms of eating disorders.

Food, exercise, weight loss, body image, health, and control are the obsessions of a teenager with an eating disturbance. The key word in that last sentence is *obsession*. Teenagers, by virtue of their developmental life stage, are more sensitive to their weight, body image, and overall looks. This hypersensitivity and preoccupation can be misinterpreted as a disorder. Yet teens with eating disorders are even more consumed with their body image and eating than average teenagers are. Their conversations, behaviors, attitudes, desires, and time all center around the disorder.

1.2 MYTHS ABOUT EATING DISORDERS

Eating disorders are only a female issue. This myth is damaging because it leads people to overlook and not recognize the symptoms presented in a male with an eating disorder. While eating disorders among females outnumber males almost seven to one, that doesn't mean this is exclusively a female issue. It's best not to read gender into the signs and symptoms of eating disorders (unless specifically noted in this book). In a later chapter, we'll look specifically at eating disorders in males.

A health care professional will uncover whether or not my child has an eating disorder during routine medical exams. People often deny having problems or engaging in behaviors that are indicative of an eating disorder. And medical professionals see teenagers infrequently. During those short visits, any fluctuations in weight can be dismissed as normal adolescent growth. Unless a medical professional is specifically looking for an eating disorder or is tipped off by a concerned parent, the disorder can easily be overlooked.

Eating disorders are just about looks and food. While body image may often factor into the epistemology of an eating disorder, most times the disorder involves much more. A teenager with an eating disorder can also be struggling with emotional issues such as depression, abuse, control issues, low self-esteem, fear and anxiety, obsessive-compulsive disorder, or identity struggles.

Eating disorders are a choice teenagers make. This myth goes hand-in-hand with the one that says a teen with an eating disorder can choose to stop—by just eating. I once had a father tell me that when he discovered his daughter had an eating disorder, he drove to her college, took her out to dinner, and told her he wasn't leaving until she ate everything he'd ordered for her. His premise was that she'd *chosen* to enter into these habits, so she could also choose to stop. In truth, an eating disorder can develop over a long period of time and is comprised of a complicated enmeshment of biological and psychological issues.

You can tell if people have an eating disorder if they're over- or underweight. There are many people who suffer from an eating disorder and tend to be within 5 to 10 pounds of an acceptable weight. Some eating disorders, over time, can result in an extreme weight shift. But often during adolescence, it would be difficult to identify teenagers with an eating disorder based on their appearance alone—especially at the onset of an eating disorder. The converse is also true: There are many overweight and underweight teens who don't struggle with eating disorders at all. Someone who struggles with his weight may not necessarily struggle with an eating disorder. It's also important to note that a dieting teenager may not be dealing with an eating disorder. But when teenagers go on diets, it should be a matter of concern and should be monitored by a knowledgeable adult.

Some eating disorders aren't life-threatening. Some people believe that anorexia nervosa is the only eating disorder that's life-threatening. In actuality, all eating disorders can be. The practices of any eating disorder—from vomiting and abusing laxatives to excessive exercise and eating limited foods to non-foods—can lead to life-threatening consequences. These abusive eating patterns can lead to gastrointestinal problems, immunity issues, cardiac stress, fluid and electrolyte imbalances, and a host of other physiological issues that, when left untreated, can spiral out of control and lead to death.

Guys who suffer from eating disorders usually struggle with their sexual orientation. This myth grows out of the ill-informed view that eating disorders are only a female issue and result from an individual's obsession to look thin and fashionable. Those ideas also play into a misinformed view of masculine identity. These combinations give way to this very destructive myth. The truth is that eating disorders have nothing to do with, nor do they have any correlation to, sexual orientation.

Compulsive or binge eating isn't an eating disorder. Wrong. Often the person who engages in habitual binge or compulsive eating is using food as an improper means of coping or attempting to eliminate personal pain and suffering. Therefore, it's an eating disorder.

People who purge only do so by vomiting. Purging is any action taken to eliminate any contents from the stomach or intestines. While vomiting is an easy way to accomplish this, many people who purge resort to greater means such as enemas, laxatives, insulin abuse, fasting, and excessive exercise.

Exercise is always a good thing. Some people can over-exercise, and people with eating disorders or body dissatisfaction often do. This type of exercise can cause stress fractures, injuries, spinal injuries, osteopenia or osteoporosis, amenorrhea, and even sudden death.

People cannot fully recover from having an eating disorder. Therapeutic intervention and treatment can take a long time depending on the individual and the comorbidity of issues that exist along with the eating disorder. Yet despite this long process, an individual can fully recover from an eating disorder. The best results often occur when intervention is done at the earliest onset. This is why it's important for youth workers and parents to understand and recognize the early warning signs for an eating disorder.

1.3 UNDERSTANDING ADOLESCENT PHYSICAL DEVELOPMENT

Puberty is the life stage in which physical growth becomes most pronounced and dramatic. During adolescence, boys and girls start to lose their childish looks and develop primary and secondary sex characteristics. This is brought on by the release of a number of growth and sex hormones. Boys can increase in height at a rate of 3.5 to 5 inches a year during adolescence, broadening their shoulders, rib cage, spine, and hips. A guy can also put on 50 pounds or more during puberty, increasing his body mass one and a half times and doubling its prepubescent state. Girls will also increase in body mass and height at a rate of about 2.5 to 4 inches a year. While the increased mass in guys is largely due to muscle development, for girls it's cellulite, which gives them the curvy shape of a woman.

These dramatic changes, along with the changes in primary sex characteristics, make every adolescent feel a sense of abnormality. One of the common practices (mostly unconsciously) is for teenagers to compare their physique with others', including other teens, adults, and those icons presented in the media. This comparison process helps teens navigate the stormy waters of physiological transformation, but it also causes them (even those with athletic physiques) to find flaws and feel abnormal. All teenagers have a distorted view or perception of their body image at some time during their adolescent years. And most try to control or alter their looks by dieting and exercising.

It's important for youth workers and parents to understand the dynamics of the physiological changes in a teenager (even beyond the brief description here). We need to help teens understand that no amount of weight lifting, exercise, or dieting will completely alter the form of a body that's still in the throes of change. I've watched junior high guys get into lifting programs in an attempt to sculpt their bodies. They achieve results, only to have them change in the subsequent years because their muscle mass changes. Similarly freshmen girls who diet to lose weight may only be fighting an uphill battle. Adults must reassure teenagers that their dramatic physical changes and growth, as well as their accompanying feelings of inadequacy and abnormality, are perfectly normal. If weight training is essential to a sport and weight loss is essential for healthy living, then it should be properly monitored and not done in excess.

1.4 UNDERSTANDING EATING DISORDERS

Specific eating disorders may have unique signs and symptoms, but there are some common signs and symptoms shared by all eating disorders that will be discussed later on in this book. Let's start by looking at some common factors that are present with all eating disorders.

Eating disorders are complex. Eating disorders aren't just a result of a person's desire to be thin or attractive. An eating disorder is more than just a vanity issue; it can stem from many different issues. The complexity of every eating disorder often mandates a complex solution.

Eating disorders affect males and females of every race and socioeconomic status. Worldwide medical research on eating disorders has indicated that all people groups and social statuses are susceptible.

Eating disorders fall into four categories: Anorexia nervosa, bulimia nervosa, binge eating disorder, and Eating Disorders Not Otherwise Specified (EDNOS).

Eating disorders share comorbidity with other psychological issues. Thee include, but aren't limited to, obsessive-compulsive disorders, anxiety disorders, perfectionism, paranoia, and depression.

Eating disorders have psychological and biological causes and consequences. There are some common precipitators of eating disorders:

- *Distorted Body Image.* Teens may harbor notions that their bodies aren't normal. This notion is also tied to their sense of value and esteem. Regardless of what they do, this obsessive desire to redefine their shape, image, or status is never satisfied. As a result teenagers obsess over sculpting their bodies by engaging in a dysfunctional relationship with food and exercise.

- *Need for Control.* Teens quickly learn that the first place where they can assert some sense of autonomy and control in their lives is over their mouths. This is why many preteens and junior highers go through a "swearing stage." They think they appear more grown-up if they use foul language. They also learn they can choose the time and place to do that, thus exercising control and secrecy. That same desire for control and autonomy factors into eating disorders. When a teen feels as though life is out of control (pervasive feelings of oppression, stress, pressure, fear, and so on), they overindulge their control over eating—either by not eating or eating whatever they desire. This can also play out in a form of rebellion, which gives teenagers a sense of entitlement to eat anything, anytime or rebel against food and its effects.

- *Fill a void or mask pain.* We all feel negative feelings at times, and sometimes we may decide our feelings could be anesthetized with an ice cream sundae. The difference between that normal response and the response of someone with an eating disorder is that that behavior becomes an obsession with an addictive proponent of dependence on food or the endorphin rush created by food and purging behaviors. This inappropriate use of food to escape life's pain becomes an addiction, very similar to the cycle of an alcoholic or drug user.

Medical history, endocrinology and neurology, genetics, and nature-nurture studies are being considered as factors in developing eating disorders. While there is support that would validate each of those factors, there's no conclusive evidence that gives us a single emerging cause.

Eating disorders are life-threatening but treatable. Intervention can include, but isn't limited to, nutritional counseling, individual psychotherapy, medications, group support programs, family-based therapy, pastoral counseling, inpatient hospitalization (in severe cases), behavior modification, or a combination of many of these in an interdisciplinary approach.

1.5 FACTORS AND CAUSES OF EATING DISORDERS

It's important to remember that eating disorders are very complex. This will help us minister more effectively to teens with these disorders. Because of the complexity involved, medical and mental health professionals have uncovered multiple causes and factors that contribute to the formation of eating disorders. One isn't more prominent than another. And as a result, there cannot be a quick fix. The next sections will help us consider some of these factors.

1.5A PSYCHOLOGICAL FACTORS

Traumatic life events. Events like the death of a loved one, loss of a relationship, or a move to a new place and school may generate feelings of being out of control or inadequate. Eating and exercising can be a way of refocusing the teen's attention away from the trauma. However, an eating disorder may also develop as an unhealthy coping skill. Other types of life trauma may include physical, sexual, or emotional abuse and assault. In these cases the eating disorder becomes the coping mechanism that helps a teen escape the pain of that precipitating trauma. And in response to instances of sexual abuse, an eating disorder may be the teenager's conscious or unconscious attempt to ward off sexual onslaughts by altering the body's shape and image.

Family dysfunction. For teens living in dysfunctional families, an eating disorder becomes an attempt to feel some sense of control in their lives. This is especially true when parents or caregivers are overcontrolling or overprotective, or if they're neglectful in creating secure boundaries for the teenager. Teens may also engage in an eating disorder in an attempt to distance themselves from their parents, seek attention, or escape the feelings of being ignored or abandoned. The eating disorder often becomes a false sense of security and control.

Major life transitions. Some teens have a very difficult time with change. Change can give way to an overwhelming sense of fear. As a result, teens will turn to eating as a way of comforting and satiating the fear or overcoming change. Normal life changes such as puberty, transition from grade school to high school and then college, and issues of autonomy become too much to bear. So eating becomes the coping skill.

Overwhelming sense of failure and lack of control. Many teens who have eating disorders also have perfectionist tendencies. They try to soothe the stress, anxiety, and fear of failure through dysfunctional eating. This is evidenced in bulimic teens who eat to compensate for the stress of failing, then throw up to correct the failure, guilt, and shame they feel for bingeing.

Poor self-esteem. Teens who feel inadequate or have a distorted body image can be susceptible to an eating disorder. The eating disorder tends to be an attempt to alter their image and make them feel good about who they are. In some cases the antithesis occurs in that the overeating becomes a means of proving their lack of personal worth. Either way, these teens usually believe their self-worth or value is directly tied to their body image. The eating disorder becomes a false sense of comfort from emotional pain.

Major illness or disability. I mentioned in a previous book in this series (*What Do I Do When Teenagers Are Depressed and Contemplate Suicide?*) that chronic illness and the realization of a disability can send teens into a deep depression and may even lead to a suicide attempt. But many teens never contemplate suicide. Instead, they begin a slow process of self-destruction through an eating disorder. An obsession with eating can become a diversion from having to deal with feelings of abnormality or limited ability. The eating disorder becomes a false pursuit to regain normality and gain acceptance.

Social problems. Some teens suffer teasing or bullying, have difficulties making and maintaining friendships, and operate from a distorted view of what's socially acceptable based on the cues they take from the media. These teens will also internalize values that being thin, being beautiful, or having the perfect body will bring them success, popularity, and greater social standing. Eating becomes a way for them to change their looks and thus escape their social problems. It also becomes a false pursuit of social acceptance and approval.

Other psychological issues. As mentioned earlier, many teens with eating disorders also present with other psychological disorders. Often these psychological issues precede the eating disorder. In other words, depression or an obsessive-compulsive disorder can precipitate an eating disorder. In such cases eating disorders can be part of teenagers' attempts to cope, gain control, or comfort themselves.

1.5B GENETICS AND FAMILIAL FACTORS

Continual research is being conducted to determine if genetic, biochemical, neurological, endocrine, and physiological factors are connected to eating disorders. Some studies have shown that anorexia and bulimia are statistically more prevalent among family members.[10] Studies on twins also give some indication that there may be a genetic component that preconditions a teenager toward eating disorders. A recent study showed a 50 percent occurrence of eating disorders among identical twins and a 10 percent occurrence among fraternal twins.[11] These studies don't conclude that eating disorders are genetic, but they do show a possible connection. A key variable in twin studies is the environment. Twins usually live in the same household. Therefore, while they obviously share the same genetics, they also share the same environment and culture. These factors could play into the development of eating disorders as well.

The brain is the controlling organ over appetite and eating regulation. A logical conclusion can be made that dysfunctions in the brain can result in eating disorders. In a person who doesn't have an eating disorder, food—or a lack of it—triggers the release of chemicals that elevate or decrease appetite. Some studies have shown a connection between bulimia and the body's ability to use and produce tryptophan and serotonin, which are both essential to healthy nutrition and emotional stability.[12] These studies are showing links between eating disorders and brain functions, body chemicals, and hormones.

While behavioral modifications—such as regulating diet or learning self-discipline and self-control—are essential to the treatment of an eating disorder, scientists are coming to the conclusion that there may be other pharmaceutical ways to treat these disorders. As of this writing, there's only one specific medication designed to treat bulimia (Fluoxetine). Most of the prescriptive drugs used in the therapeutic treatment of eating disorders target the coexisting psychological disorders, such as depression, obsessive-compulsive disorders, or anxiety.

1.5C CULTURAL FACTORS

Body weight and beauty are viewed differently from culture to culture. In Western cultures there tends to be a greater preoccupation with thinness than in societies and cultures in the other two-thirds of the world. The primary precipitator of an eating disorder may also vary from culture to culture. In Hong Kong and India, for example, eating disorders may take root from a desire to be holy. Religious zealots go on extended fasts or have extremely restrictive diets that can result in eating disorders.[13]

Yet apart from religious purity, there's still been an increase in the occurrence of eating disorders among non-Westerners. The speculation is that technology has brought about a blurring of cultural values so Western cultural norms—including those related to the ideal body shape—are now being adopted elsewhere.[14] A study of a pre-television culture of Pacific Islanders revealed they had little-to-no concern about body image. In fact, a thin person was presumed to be sickly. But when this culture adopted modern technology, cases of eating disorders began to surface, and young girls started believing they needed to look like the icons they saw presented in the media.[15]

The media tends to be a cultural marker that impacts eating disorders. Many studies have been done on the effects of fashion and fitness magazines, television, and films, as they either reflect our culture's belief that ultra-thinness is the only acceptable form of beauty, or they promote thinness by using models who rarely represent the majority of the population. The results are not only an increased desire and drive for thinness among adolescents (especially girls), but also body dissatisfaction among all adolescents—girls and guys.

In her book *Teenage Girls*, Ginny Olson points out the following cultural facts:[16]

- In order to be a runway model, a girl needs to be at least 5'9" tall, long-legged, and have a long neck and broad shoulders. Less than five percent of the population fits these dimensions.
- The probability of a person having the same physical dimensions as the iconic Barbie doll is 1 in 100,000. And the probability of a guy having Ken's physical dimensions are 1 in 50.
- Given the choice, 80 percent of three-to-five year olds prefer to play with a doll that's thin because "It's more fun than playing with a doll that looks fat."
- Before the 1960s, female models and performers in America weighed only 7 percent less than the average woman. By the 1970s, they weighed 15 percent less.

- Of "normal dieters," 35 percent progress to pathological dieting. And of those, 20 to 25 percent progress to partial or full-syndrome eating disorders.[17]

To add fuel to the fire, there's been a rise in many pro-anorexia and pro-bulimia Web sites. Often called "Pro-Ana" or "Pro-Mia" sites, they advocate anorexia and bulimia as lifestyle choices, rather than psychological and medical disorders. The popularity of these sites is greater in the United Kingdom, but it's rapidly growing in the United States and other countries where teens have more access to the Internet. The creators of these sites believe they're providing "thinspiration" through pictures and stories, as well as tips for how to binge and purge better, how to deceive health professionals and concerned adults, the best excuses to use when covering one's eating behaviors, and even crash diet ideas. They also present anti-medical warning messages and tout that those messages are false or are scare tactics to infringe on the individual's right to do what they wish with their bodies.

These Web sites also exalt ultra-thin celebrity icons as examples to follow. Some give tips on how to overcome hunger, for example, instigating personal conflicts so the anxiety generated from the conflict keeps the teen from eating; inflicting personal pain and self-mutilation whenever hunger strikes; repeating mantras such as, "An imperfect body reflects an imperfect person"; and drinking vinegar to satiate appetite. These destructive Web sites attract younger teens who are struggling with eating and body image issues. Chat rooms and social networking, blogs, and message boards coach onlookers with stories and tips on how to be a "better anorexic." One such network posts destructive rules and regulations to follow, such as "The 10 Thin Commandments":

1. If you aren't thin, you aren't attractive.
2. Being thin is more important than being healthy.
3. You must buy clothes, cut your hair, take laxatives, starve yourself, do anything to make yourself look thinner.
4. Thou shall not eat without feeling guilty.
5. Thou shall not eat fattening food without punishing oneself afterwards.
6. Thou shall count calories and restrict intake accordingly.
7. What the scale says is the most important thing.
8. Losing weight is good/gaining weight is bad.
9. You can never be too thin.
10. Being thin and not eating are signs of true will power and success.

While many prominent search engines have banned these sites, their popularity increases and it becomes more difficult to monitor them. Youth workers must be aware of these sites and become a more powerful voice in the lives of hurting teens. Teenagers who gravitate to and are influenced by these sites often feel very alone and seek relationships with others who are also in pain.

Along with our culture's fixation on appearance, there's an obsession with athletic performance. Many teenagers believe they must be incredible athletes in order to qualify for college scholarships or be scouted by a top school. In addition, many teens have been pushed since they were children to chase the pipe dream of becoming wealthy, elite professional athletes. As a result, they get caught in a rut of training and performance. They become at-risk for eating disorders—especially if their sports are individualized and have weight requirements (such as gymnastics, wrestling, boxing, skating, diving, martial arts, and so on) or are high endurance (such as track and field or swimming). The risk is enhanced when coaches and other adults push these teenagers to believe that a lower body weight will enhance their performance. Often these coaches and trainers are more concerned about winning and performance than the well-being of the athletes.

There are many opportunities for girls to be active in athletics, and many of them can find careers in fields where physical fitness is required. Because of the pressures that our culture puts on women regarding looks and performance, there's been a lot of concern about the prevention and rehabilitation of physical issues that could harm the female athlete. The Female Athlete Triad Coalition was formed in 2002 to address interrelated medical issues that affect female athletes, including eating disorders, amenorrhea, and osteoporosis. The Coalition strives to prevent these issues through advocacy, education, international leadership, public policy, and research.[18] Increasing the awareness of eating disorders, amenorrhea, and osteoporosis among female athletes and the people who work with them has become the concern of many athletic organizations and associations throughout the world, including the International Olympic Committee (IOC).

1.6 TYPES OF EATING DISORDERS

The American Psychological Association has categorized eating disorders into four major categories:

1.6A ANOREXIA NERVOSA

This eating disorder is typified by the teen starving himself or herself. This form of self-starvation can often include binge eating and purging. Because of the purging component, most untrained youth workers may see this as bulimia. (We will discuss bulimia more in the next section.) The difference between the two disorders lies in the amount of weight loss and some practices among the teen with the disorder. Anorexics weigh less than 85 percent of the expected normative weight for their age and height. Binge eating and purging may be a part of their behavior, but the difference is that they're at a dangerously low weight and don't see it.

Typically anorexia is marked by self-starvation. The term comes from the Greek *orexis*, meaning "appetite," preceded by the Greek root *ana*, meaning "without." Thus, when translated, anorexia means "without appetite." The Greek *nervosa* means to be nervous as an implied agitation over something. So the translation of the entire term *anorexia nervosa* means "a psychological nervousness that leaves one without appetite." While that may be the literal translation, we know this disorder is much more than just a loss of appetite.

Anorexic teens are consumed with their weight and body image. They venture into destructive eating habits, such as counting calories, eliminating foods from their diet, eating smaller and smaller portions, chewing but never swallowing their food, and not eating at all or fasting. When done consistently over time, all of these behaviors will cause someone to lose a dramatic amount of weight and eventually that person will be far below the normal weight for her height and age. Most anorexics have the ongoing mindset that they're fat because they have issues with their body image. As a result a very emaciated anorexic teen will diet, over-exercise, and even fast because of a fear of gaining weight or becoming "fatter."

According to the *American Psychiatric Association's Diagnostic and Statistical Manual of Mental Disorders*, Fourth Edition Text Revision (DSM-IV-TR), the criteria for anorexia nervosa are as follows:[19]

1. A refusal to maintain body weight at or above a minimally normal weight for age and height (for example, weight loss leading to a maintenance of body weight less than 85 percent of that expected, or failure to make expected weight gain during period of growth, leading to body weight less than 85 percent of that expected).
2. Intense fear of gaining weight or becoming fat, even though underweight.
3. Disturbance in the way in which one's body weight or shape is experienced, undue influence of body weight or shape on self-evaluation, or denial of the seriousness of the current low body weight.

The DSM-IV-TR also categorizes anorexia nervosa into two categories or types. The first is called the "Restrictive Type" indicating that the teen doesn't engage in any binge-eating or purging behaviors. The second is the "Binge-Eating/Purging Type" where the teen engages regularly in these activities.

Teens with anorexia nervosa have a distorted view of not only their bodies, but also their "selves." Their self-esteem and self-worth run low. In addition many anorexics can be perfectionists and obsessive. This combination makes a teen prime for anorexia. The end result is that teens starve themselves in order to be accepted or feel more valuable. Their perfectionist tendencies make them feel as though they're never thin enough, even though they can realistically assess that other teens look gaunt or emaciated if they're below the normal weight expectancy for their height and age. Anorexic adolescents may even attempt to convince their friends that they're at a good weight (not too fat or skinny), even though these friends don't have an ideal body. Yet the anorexics cannot apply these same criteria to themselves.

Some symptoms of anorexia may be seen long before the anorexic starts to lose weight. Certain tendencies, behaviors, attitudes, and values are the first signs that should raise immediate concerns. Some of the symptoms of anorexia nervosa include the following psychological, behavioral, and physiological signs.

PSYCHOLOGICAL SIGNS

- Perfectionist tendencies
- May start comparing their body image with others and have distorted self-images
- Fear of gaining weight and an obsessive, out-of-control concern with body image and weight
- Constantly feel as though they're fat or overweight despite dramatic weight loss
- Personality changes that reflect withdrawn, isolationist tendencies
- Display obsessive-compulsive ideations (in other words, focusing on a single body part [such as the arms or face] as the representation of the entire body; anorexic teens may diet excessively because they believe their cheeks are too fat or their ankles look too big, and so on)
- Lack of concentration and an inability to stay focused
- May experience bouts of depression, low self-esteem, paranoia, and suicidal ideation

BEHAVIORAL SIGNS

- Often have difficulties finishing a meal; food or the smell of food may become nauseating to them
- May avoid situations and events where food is being served (this is often the reason why students with eating disorders don't come to meals at camps or retreats)
- Refuse to eat or deny being hungry; may skip meals and make excuses for not eating
- May develop abnormal eating practices, such as eating un-usually small portions, weighing foods, or chewing but not swallowing their food (parents may find food spit into nap-kins, or anorexic teens may excuse themselves to discard chewed food)
- Over-exercising can become an obsession in that teens may become paranoid if they miss their routine. They'll exercise multiple times a day to the point of physically hurting their bodies. They'll even attempt to exercise when they're ill or have no strength.
- Constantly talk about weight, body image, or exercising; con-stantly look in the mirror to check the flaws which they be-lieve define them
- Limit food intake to low-calorie foods; become very con-cerned with counting and restricting calories
- May categorize foods as "good," "safe," or "bad," and this cataloging becomes a regular part of their conversations
- Withdraw from family and friends; isolate themselves and becoming more secretive
- May pretend to have food allergies; become picky eaters or decide to become vegetarian or vegan eaters
- May wear baggy clothes or many layers of clothes to hide their bodies

PHYSIOLOGICAL SIGNS

- Thin and emaciated physique: The teen may lose weight rapidly (as evidenced by their baggy clothes). As weight loss progresses, the teen will look gaunt and skeletal.
- May evidence signs of self-mutilation, such as wearing clothing that covers their arms and legs to hide marks. May show signs of self-harm, such as scratches, lacerations, burns, scarring, and so on. Remember, anorexics can resort to painful extremes to rid themselves of hunger.
- Muscle weakness or loss: When there's no body fat left to burn, the muscles begin to deteriorate. Anorexic teens may have difficulty lifting heavy objects or performing strenuous tasks.
- Anemia: Blood is affected by the lack of iron and other minerals it needs to be healthy. When deprived of food, the blood fails to be enriched.
- Chronic fatigue. Even if they get plenty of rest, they'll always feel tired because their body isn't getting the appropriate fuel (nutrients, vitamins, and minerals) it needs to run effectively.
- Dizziness and fainting
- Headaches
- Hair loss and brittle nails: Because of the lack of nutrition, their hair may become brittle, break, and even begin to fall out. Their nails may also become very brittle and break a lot.
- Dry and yellowish skin due to malnourishment. Prior to this the skin on their arms and legs may look purplish resulting from poor blood flow.
- Low blood pressure and body temperature (the teen will always feel cold, even on warm days). This can also result in a slower heart rhythm and respiration.
- Exhibit the growth of lanugo, a soft, white, downy hair on their arms and chest. This happens mostly to anorexics who are near emaciation. The hair grows as a body's protective measure to maintain its normal temperature. When a

teenager drops weight in a dramatic way and keeps it off, that teen's body may not have enough insulation normally found in the body fat to maintain a healthy body temperature. Thus, the body compensates by creating its own "blanket." Lanugo is normally seen on newborn infants. It develops as an insulating mechanism in the mother's womb. Lanugo usually goes away as the infant nurses and maintains a healthy weight due to proper nutrition. Lanugo isn't common past infancy, and it's a strong sign of anorexia.

- Gastric problems: Severe constipation or chronic diarrhea
- Bone and joint pain
- Slow wound healing
- Amenorrhea: Missing three or more consecutive menstrual periods. Low body weight interrupts many normal hormonal functions, including menstruation and ovulation. Mothers tend to get the first hint of this symptom because they're usually the ones who purchase feminine hygiene products for their household. If a teenage girl is hiding an eating disorder and isn't having her period, she won't need to use these feminine products.
- The hormone reduction brought on by an eating disorder usually evidences itself as a loss of sexual drive or appetite in a guy.

1.6B BULIMIA NERVOSA

Bulimia comes from the Greek root *bous*, referring to oxen, and *limos*, which means "hunger." The word literally means "to have the hunger of an ox." This term is used because bulimic teens usually binge to excess and then attempt to purge their systems of the calories through a number of unhealthy means. Unlike anorexics, bulimics eat. Their weight isn't excessively low like that of the anorexic, but they share a fear of gaining too much weight, a distorted body image, and low self-esteem.

Usually a teen with bulimia can go undetected because they *do* eat and may even have a normative body weight. Like anorexia, bulimia is very secretive. The teen with this disorder lives with a lot of guilt and shame over her eating behaviors and a fear of being found out. The bulimic teen may eat too much (or *believe* he or she has eaten too much) and then vomit it all. As a result, a bulimic can become deprived of the necessary nutrition to stay healthy. At times the bulimic may not immediately purge, or she may use methods of purging that are slower acting. Eventually this could lead to weight gain because the calories from her binge eating have already been ingested.

As with any eating disorder, food, weight, exercise, and body image become the obsessions of the bulimic. These teens often define themselves by their physical flaws and imperfections. They compare themselves to those they find more attractive or believe to have perfect bodies. These continual comparisons can lead to an addictive cycle of inappropriate eating in which the teen will binge eat and then feel guilty, resulting in the purging behaviors.

Binge eating almost takes on the form of an addiction in which the teens cannot gauge limitations or stop the eating behaviors. They may eat large quantities of foods in a short period of time, and they often feel as though the eating is out of their control—they can't stop it. A bulimic teen can consume between 3,000 and 5,000 calories in an hour. A binge-eating episode can consist of consuming one or two gallons of ice cream, boxes of crackers, bags of candies or cookies, dozens of donuts, an entire cake, or many combinations of these foods in excess—all in one sitting. And even when the bulimic teen feels ill or painfully full from the amount of food taken in, he'll continue to consume these foods.

Sometimes binge eating can be known as "hyperphagia" or excessive overeating. Hyperphagia is usually associated with medical abnormalities in the hypothalamus, resulting in an uncontrolled appetite that causes the individual to overeat. But in the case of the bulimic, hyperphagia may refer only to ingesting more than normal amounts of food or eating to excess. Purging then becomes the means of relief from the discomfort caused by binge eating.

The most common form of purging is self-induced vomiting. Bulimics may put their fingers down their throats or resort to other means, such as swallowing raw eggs or drinking household substances (cooking oils or medications like ipecac), to induce vomiting. They may also drink liters of soda pop after bingeing in order to provoke a gag reflex. When vomiting occurs, the body releases endorphins (the body's natural opiate) that act as an analgesic, numbing the pain and creating an exhilarating or euphoric feeling. Sometimes it can also create a false sense of power or control. This endorphin rush becomes the response or "high" that the bulimic seeks after binge eating.

Other forms of purging can include the misuse and abuse of laxatives and diuretics, frequent enemas, and using saunas as a way of purging calories. However, none of these methods actually purge any calories; they only dehydrate the body. The water loss causes the teen to weigh less, thereby giving the immediate illusion of weight loss. In the long run, however, the body can become bloated as it retains more fluid in order to compensate for the dehydration. This cycle can be dangerous. Furthermore, calorie absorption occurs in the small intestine, whereas laxatives affect only the large intestine by assisting in the elimination of stool and undigested foods. So this type of purging is also ineffective. Because all bodily functions and systems are dependent upon water, teens who dehydrate their systems in this manner run the risk of severe medical complications—even death.

A teen can also have a non-purging form of bulimia in which he'll still binge eat, but it's often followed by fasting and over-exercising as a means of eliminating calories and controlling weight gain. Frequent dieting (successive days of eating little or no food) followed by bingeing becomes the pattern of a non-purging bulimic. Girls who frequently diet are 12 times as likely to binge as girls who don't diet.[20]

The DSM-IV-TR's criteria for bulimia are as follows:[21]

1. Recurrent episodes of binge eating. An episode of binge eating is characterized by both of the following:
   a. Eating, in a discrete period of time (for example, within any two-hour period), an amount of food that is definitely larger than what most people would eat during a similar period of time and under similar circumstances
   b. A sense of lack of control over eating during the episode (for example, a feeling that one cannot stop eating or control what or how much one is eating)
2. Recurrent inappropriate compensatory behaviors in order to prevent weight gain, such as self-induced vomiting; misuse of laxatives, diuretics, enemas, or other medications; fasting; or excessive exercise.

3. The binge-eating and inappropriate compensatory behaviors both occur, on average, at least twice a week for three months.
4. Self-evaluation is unduly influenced by body shape and weight.
5. The disturbance does not occur exclusively during episodes of anorexia nervosa.

Teenagers who are involved in high-profile activities or are required to be in good shape (for example, dancers, performers, athletes, and so on) tend to be at higher risk than others. Some of the symptoms of bulimia are shared by all eating disorders. (Those are discussed later in this book.) But there are some unique psychological, behavioral, and physiological symptoms that mark bulimia.

PSYCHOLOGICAL SIGNS

- Strong preoccupation with body shape and weight
- Negative self-image and a distorted perspective of their own body size and shape
- Low self-esteem and an inability to believe they're valuable, loved, and accepted
- Guilt, shame, fear, panic, and anxiety are frequent emotional states

BEHAVIORAL SIGNS

- Secretive behaviors and disappearing for short amounts of time. Bulimic teens will binge eat when they're alone. This is often done in the middle of the night or in the privacy of their bedroom or bathroom. Generally, bulimia requires a great deal of time spent alone or in isolation. A violation of this boundary will make the affected teen agitated or uneasy.

- Always frequenting the bathroom immediately after a meal to purge. They may run water or make noise to cover the sounds of throwing up.
- Hoarding food. Parents may find food wrappers and containers, along with hidden food stashes, in the teen's bedroom (under the bed, between the mattresses, in dresser drawers, in closets) or car. Parents may also discover that food is disappearing without account.
- Eating an unusual amount of food with relatively little change in weight.
- Excessive exercising or an obsession with working out.
- Money issues: The teen may spend large amounts of money while secretly buying food or making fast-food runs. The bulimic teen will always ask for money or resort to stealing (just like in the case of any substance addiction) so they can buy food. When confronted, the teen will make up stories, lie, or be unable to give an account for their money.

PHYSIOLOGICAL SIGNS

- Smell of vomit. They may attempt to cover it up by wearing strong perfume, chewing gum or mints, or smoking. They may also try to cover the smell in the bathroom or bedroom by burning candles or using strong air fresheners.
- They may frequently change their clothes because of soiling due to vomiting.
- Fingers and knuckles may be calloused, cut, or scarred. This is from putting their fingers down their throats to induce vomiting. Gastric acids can chap hands, and teens may cut their fingers on their teeth as a result of the force exerted from projectile vomiting.
- Swollen, bloodshot eyes or broken blood vessels or capillaries in and around the eyes from the force exerted by vomiting

- Raspy voice or hoarseness as a result of damage done to the vocal cords from vomiting; may often be accompanied by chronic sore throat
- Swollen glands in the neck and under the jaw, as well as sialadenosis (inflammation of the salivary glands, which makes the teen's face and cheeks look puffy or chipmunk-like) caused by constant vomiting
- Mouth and dental problems caused by vomiting and acid reflux, including chapped lips and mouth, erosion of tooth enamel, cavities, and a foul smell from rotting teeth and gum disease
- Irritable bowels, constipation, and diarrhea resulting from the abuse of laxatives and diuretics
- Dehydration from purging fluids
- Malnutrition
- Kidney problems may result from abusing diuretics. Diuretics can cause an imbalance in electrolytes and low levels of potassium, which can also result in cardiac arrhythmia and a host of other heart problems.

1.6C BINGE-EATING DISORDER

Sometimes referred to as "compulsive overeating," this disorder is similar to bulimia in that the teenager has an uncontrolled obsession with binge eating. And the binge-eating episodes follow the same description as bulimia. However, the difference is that the binge-eating teen doesn't purge, diet, fast, or exercise afterward, resulting in a grossly overweight or obese teen.

Overweight teens may have difficulty assimilating into a youth group. Besides feeling bad about themselves, having low self-esteem, and believing they're abnormal, obese teenagers battle being unaccepted, teased, bullied, and ridiculed. Often these teens experience this same kind of treatment within their own youth groups. People who work with teenagers need to understand that helping these teens means creating a safe environment. Unfortunately, binge-eaters often try to find solace in food.

The DSM-IV-TR criteria for binge-eating disorders are as follows:[22]

1. Recurrent episodes of binge eating, which are characterized by
   - Eating a larger amount of food than normal during a short period of time (within any two-hour period)
   - A lack of control during the binge episode (in other words, the feeling that one cannot stop eating)
2. Binge-eating episodes are associated with three or more of the following:
   - Eating until feeling uncomfortably full
   - Eating large amounts of food when not physically hungry
   - Eating much more rapidly than normal
   - Eating alone because you're embarrassed by how much you're eating
   - Feeling disgusted, depressed, or guilty after overeating
3. Marked distress regarding binge eating
4. Binge eating occurs, on average, at least two days a week for six months.
5. Binge eating isn't associated with the regular use of inappropriate compensatory behavior (such as purging, excessive exercise, and so on), and it doesn't occur exclusively during the course of bulimia nervosa or anorexia nervosa

Some of the physiological complications that result from binge eating and obesity are

- High blood pressure and heart disease
- Diabetes

- High cholesterol
- Gallbladder disease
- Sleep problems
- Muscle, bone, and joint pain
- Headaches
- Digestive problems

1.6D EATING DISORDERS NOT OTHERWISE DESIGNATED (EDNOD)

This category of eating disorders encompasses all other eating disorders that don't meet the criteria of being anorexia nervosa or bulimia nervosa.

Excessive Exercise (May also be called "compulsive exercise," "obligatory exercise," or "anorexia athletica.") Many times this occurs in tandem with another eating disorder, but it can also be experienced alone. Compulsive exercise can become an addiction and have the same effects as one. Teens who exercise excessively have misdirected motives for why they put their bodies through this rigor:

- They're often frustrated with their body image or looks.
- They feel a sense of weakness or lack of control that they believe exercise will overcome.
- They may have low or poor self-esteem.
- They use exercise as a means of escaping emotional pain.

The phenomenon behind excessive exercise is that there comes a point when the teen doesn't see exercise as being optional but essential and necessary to her survival. Teens who experience this addiction tend to feel panic, anxiety, depression, guilt, nervousness, or even dread if they miss or cannot exercise. This can largely be due to the endorphin rush that often accompanies a rigorous work out.

Endorphins act as the body's natural analgesic by minimizing pain, relieving stress and anxiety, and creating a euphoria or sense of well being. Endorphins become the drug of choice, and teens who over-exercise quickly learn that a daily, prolonged exercise schedule gives them the needed escape from life's cares. Like any addiction, a teen who has an exercise disorder may miss school, ignore essential responsibilities, abandon or isolate herself from friends and family, and default on social obligations in order to exercise. The effects of excessive exercise can include chronic exhaustion, decreased performance in other life skills, loss of appetite, gastrointestinal problems, headaches, immune deficiency, respiratory problems, cardio problems, weight loss, decrease in muscle tone, muscle damage, bone and joint damage, as well as a host of psychological damages that typically accompany addictions.

Some common signs of an exercise addiction include:

- Isolation and withdrawal from others—especially while exercising. Teens who excessively exercise do it alone.
- Like an eating disorder, teens may become secretive about exercising by not disclosing what they're doing, exercising in isolated locations like the garage or attic, and waking up in the middle of the night to exercise without being discovered.
- Obsessed with weight loss, body image, or caloric intake and expenditure
- Constantly follow and hold to the same rigid patters and routines of exercise
- They exercise for more than two hours repeatedly throughout the day, every day.
- They continuously exercise beyond their pain threshold and exercise even when they're ill or injured. They may also have physical injuries.
- They skip school, work, or social plans so they can work out.

Adonis Complex. A group of Harvard professors and researchers coined this term after they noticed an increase in the occurrence of this complex obsession among men (starting in adolescence) and other related problems regarding body image. In Greek mythology the god Adonis' perfect body and strength epitomized the ideal of masculinity. Thus, *Adonis Complex* refers to the growing obsession that many men have with achieving that ideal and the methods they use to do it. This includes over-exercising, compulsive weightlifting, steroid use and abuse, dysfunctional eating patterns, and body or muscle dysmorphia.

Muscle dysmorphia is an obsessive-compulsive disorder in which an individual (usually male) believes his physique is small, weak, and underdeveloped. No matter what he does, he believes he's still too small—never muscular enough. And the obsession comes about as he tries to correct this matter through unhealthy means. In some ways this disorder is the opposite of anorexia. Whereas anorexia affects mostly women who believe they're never small enough, muscle dysmorphia affects many men who believe they're never muscularly big enough. This is why the disorder is sometimes called "bigorexia nervosa" or "reverse anorexia nervosa" by popular culture. Most sufferers of the Adonis Complex are very physically fit and muscularly defined. But this body image disorder, particularly in teenage guys, is associated with a culturally warped view of masculine identity as being big and strong. Male teens with an Adonis Complex will attempt to become the ideal man almost constantly, but they always find themselves falling short. This relentless striving becomes dangerous when it leads teens to take steroids or muscle defining drugs and supplements and eat dysfunctionally—even when they're fully aware of the lethal consequences of their actions.

Like the other eating and body image disorders discussed in this book, muscle dysmorphic teens exercise excessively even when they're injured. Their preoccupation with the inadequacies of their physique and their all-consuming thoughts of correcting it interfere with their school and work performances, relationships, coping skills, and normal life functions and pleasures. They may often feel paranoid, believing that everyone is judging their physique, seeing them as less than manly, or perceiving them to be weak individuals. They might also become obsessed with eating the "right foods." Over time this may lead to a more restricted diet with increased vitamin supplementation.

Like other eating disorders, teens with an Adonis Complex become stressed and anxious if their eating routines are inhibited or altered. Some symptoms, not mentioned above, may include:

- A fear of taking off their shirts or disrobing in public because they're afraid of being ridiculed for their smaller size. In reality their obsessive weightlifting may make them very defined or bigger than the norm, which often draws attention to them. But teens with this disorder mistakenly believe this attention is actually ridicule. As a result they may avoid going to beaches, swimming pools, locker rooms, and so on.
- Wearing baggy clothes in an attempt to hide their physiques
- They may suffer injuries from working out too much, but they go untreated.
- Their conversation topics deviate very little from working out to body shapes and sizes. They may constantly compare themselves to bigger guys—whom they typically find in bodybuilding magazines.
- They may avoid going to events where food is served, or they may bring their own food in the form of supplements or

powders (like creatine or protein powders) that can be rehydrated.

- They may engage in binge eating and purging.
- Spending large amounts of money on bodybuilding supplies, personal weights, grooming products, supplements, and even drugs like anabolic steroids
- If a teenage guy is using steroids, there may be additional symptoms, such as blurred vision, hallucinations, bloating and fluid retention, acne or skin problems, dizziness, muscle cramping and joint pain, jaundice (yellowing of the skin and eyes), loss of sex drive, mood swings and depression, and aggressive behaviors accompanied by anger and rage (sometimes termed "roid rage").

Orthorexia Nervosa. This is an obsession with eating only the right foods or, in the mind of the person with this disorder, eating only natural, healthy foods. Orthorexia nervosa goes beyond healthy eating and becomes a life obsession that mirrors some of the symptoms of addiction. Teenagers who present with this disorder are more than just health conscious—they're engaged in a very dangerous, life-threatening eating disorder. This food obsession, like others, interferes with daily functioning, healthy relationships, proper coping skills, and good mental and physical health.

Orthorexia nervosa is a relatively new discovery, entering the limelight of the medical and mental health community in the mid '90s. The term comes from the Greek root *ortho*, meaning "proper, right, or correct," and *orexis*, meaning "appetite." Orthorexia usually begins during adolescence when a teenager chooses to become a vegetarian. As the obsession continues, the teen becomes vegan, and then her diet becomes even more restricted to just a few foods. It's important to note that vegetarian or vegan lifestyles aren't unhealthy or orthorexic.

However, orthorexia in teens usually begins with a misdirected understanding of restricted eating.

An orthorexic teen, unlike an anorexic teen, isn't concerned with the *quantity* of food consumed but with the quality of the food. Orthorexic teens can restrict their diets to just a few acceptable foods. The criteria in deciding which foods are "proper" is part of the obsession. Teens may refuse to eat anything that isn't organically grown and become consumed with knowing how something is treated as it grows. Sometimes the disorder includes an aversion to eating anything cooked, making raw food the only acceptable or "right foods" to eat. Given that, an orthorexic can eat their fill of the "appropriate" foods, even if they dislike them.

Like an anorexic, the orthorexic will begin to lose a lot of weight and will believe this result is congruent to pure, natural, healthy living. As I mentioned earlier, this disorder, like many of the other eating disorders, usually starts during adolescence. The teen may announce to her family and friends that she's restricted her diet to a vegan diet. She may criticize the family's meals and decline to eat unhealthy foods. Some parents interpret this behavior as just a phase, or they believe the teen is becoming more of a picky eater.

As the disorder progresses, the teen may begin to lose weight, become emaciated, suffer from vitamin deficiencies, and a host of other physical consequences brought on by starvation. This disorder usually has many of the same symptoms as anorexia, which leads many health officials to believe it's just a modification of anorexia. But there's one distinct difference—the teen eats a lot.

Some signs that would indicate orthorexia are as follows:

- They care more about the types of foods they eat than the flavors or the pleasure of the food itself.
- They categorize foods as being either "good" or "bad" and constantly reevaluate—ever diminishing the foods they once believed to be "good."
- They feel empowered. Thus, they're likely to not only display an increase in self-esteem and superiority, but also appear more joyful and happy when—and because—they're sticking to their diet and eating the right foods.
- They compromise relationships and life responsibilities to plan out their meals or avoid eating something they believe they shouldn't.
- They become more and more restrictive with their diets.
- They fear there will be negative or harmful outcomes if they eat the wrong foods.
- They become obsessed with researching foods, including calling food companies, growers, restaurants, and processors to ask about hidden ingredients, chemicals, or the possibilities of contaminants in their food.
- They believe they're living a healthy lifestyle—similar to a teen with anorexia.

Pica. This disorder is categorized by the ingestion of nonnutritive substances for a period of one or more months, by someone who's at an age in which this behavior is developmentally inappropriate. A person with this eating disorder ingests, chews on, and swallows non-nutritional or non-food materials, including—but not limited to—dirt, sand, clay, chalk, paste and glue, plastic, wood, paper, pencil erasers, rubber bands, glass, stones and pebbles, soaps and laundry detergents, cigarette butts, coffee grounds, string, metal objects like paper clips and needles, hair, fingernail and toenail clippings, and even feces.

Pica is largely unknown because it's often under-reported or not understood to be a disorder at all. Many times it's viewed as being a symptom of some other problem or a ploy for attention. Pica isn't gender-bound, meaning as many males present with the problem as females do. And it doesn't have a common age boundary—children, adolescents, and adults can all present with this disorder. But it's more commonly found among under-privileged and uneducated people where nutritional education and nutritious food is limited. In this case pica is the result of hunger and malnutrition.

Sometimes pica is also associated with mental retardation or autism. And while there is some evidence that points to pica developing in younger pregnant girls as a result of a mineral deficiency in their systems, this finding isn't conclusive or verifiable.

Many mental health professionals are beginning to believe that when a person without brain dysfunction has this condition (which is rare), it should be categorized as an obsessive-compulsive disorder more than an eating disorder. Long-term effects can include toxicity from ingesting poisonous materials; GI tract complications such as ulcers, perforations, and hemorrhaging; bowel problems, intestinal obstructions, and bezoars or masses that can become trapped in the gastrointestinal system; infection from ingesting contaminated materials; parasitic infestation from ingesting material such as soil, which hosts roundworms and other parasites; and dental abrasions, tooth fractures, chips, and even tooth loss.

Prader-Willi Syndrome. This is a genetic disorder that causes hyperphagia, or an increase in appetite, brought about by a dysfunction of the hypothalamus. Hyperphagia doesn't allow the individual to experience satiation from hunger. As a result, the person experiences chronic hunger, which often leads to hoarding, stealing, and hiding food. It may also lead the individual to eat inappropriate foods such as pet food. Teens with Prader-Willi syndrome suffer from obesity, shortness of stature, delayed puberty, deficient muscle tone, mild mental retardation or learning disabilities, diabetes, and dental problems. They may also experience obsessive-compulsive behaviors and sleep disturbances.

Children with this disorder are most often friendly, loving, and obedient. As they grow into adolescence, they can become socially awkward, stubborn, and disobedient due to the hyperphagia. Because this is a genetic disorder, there is no way of correcting it; but a person can still live productively with this disorder, attend school, and hold a job. And some hormonal therapy can help with the issue of delayed growth. Youth workers should be aware that although it's a rare disorder, there may be a family in their parish whose obese teenager suffers from this anomaly.

Sleep-Eating Disorder. Sometimes known as "nocturnal sleep-related eating disorder" or NS-RED, this disorder combines sleepwalking with an eating disorder. People with this disorder usually get up in the middle of the night and eat without ever being consciously aware of their actions. They may even cook food while they're asleep. The late-night eating is usually characteristic of bingeing, and many times the foods consumed are high in sugars and fats, resulting in obesity or being overweight. This disorder usually affects the late-adolescent, and it's more common among women. It can be treated either pharmacologically or with thera-peutic intervention without the use of medications.

Night Eating Syndrome. This is different from NS–RED because the individual is awake when the eating occurs. Individuals with night eating syndrome tend to be obese or overweight. They also binge eat, but they're aware and awake during the bingeing episodes. Night eaters usually display daytime anorexia (won't eat at all during the day) but then eat excessively during the evening. This disorder is usually marked by insomnia, too. Many times the night eater will experience anxiety, stress, depression, and guilt.

1.7 COMMON SYMPTOMS

While specific eating disorders may have unique symptoms, almost all of them will exhibit many of the following:

- Increased weight loss or weight gain
- Preoccupation or obsession with food, exercise, body shape, image, or weight as demonstrated in their conversations, be-haviors, and attitudes
- Constant weight fluctuation within 10 to 15 pounds
- Dental problems
- Distorted body image and consciousness—they may be dis-gusted with their body shape and size and teased about their looks.
- Hair loss or brittle fingernails, along with other telltale signs of malnutrition
- Unusual or inconsistent eating habits, such as skipping meals, eating only one food, and counting calories
- Isolation and secrecy, especially (but not exclusively) sur-rounding meal times

- Mood swings, anxiety, fear, guilt, shame, and depression are common emotional markers.
- Amenorrhea in women and a diminished sex drive in males

1.8 GUYS AND EATING DISORDERS

Most people believe guys are exempt from having eating disorders. This usually comes from a societal view that guys, especially adolescent guys, are eating machines. There is a mystique that associates masculine bravado with eating a lot. Rarely do we hear about teenage guys dieting. This bravado makes it easier for a guy to hide the dysfunctional eating or causes adults to overlook the possibility of an eating disorder. When there is suspicion of an eating disorder, teenage guys and their parents are usually reluctant to seek treatment because of the societal stigma that it's a "female issue." If youth workers are going to effectively care for teenagers, they need to fight this stigma and be aware that they may encounter teenage guys who struggle with eating disorders in their own youth groups.

In addition, we're now seeing a trend in which the male body is becoming more of a hyper-sexualized marketing icon. The chiseled, perfect image of a male supermodel has begun to set the bar for not only how a man should look, but also what masculine bravado should be. This is having the same effect on males that the phenomenon of supermodel emulation has on females. Many guys attempt to become what they see.

The symptoms of eating disorders are the same regardless of the person's gender. However, one major difference is that guys can make sport of binge eating and purging, as if it's just a teenage guy thing. Many guys who are in sports that require them to make a weight category will binge and purge openly. This type of behavior is seen as another way that guys buffet their bodies in order to be strong and perform well. And often coaches will pass off the behavior as just a part of teenage masculine athletic activity and view the excessive weight loss as beneficial to the teen's performance.

Teenage guys are rarely challenged to be defined by their character qualities—especially Christian ones such as love, compassion, goodness, humbleness, patience, gentleness, and self-control—

because these characteristics are typically viewed as being feminine traits. Thus, more and more guys choose to be defined by their outward appearance. They believe that physical strength—along with a V-shape, six-pack abs, chiseled pecs, guns for arms, and athletically defined legs—makes them more acceptable as men. They aren't taught that masculinity is broader than one's physical appearance. Many teenage guys receive the same false messages that teenage girls have been receiving for years—*physical appearance defines your value and validates your gender.*

Teenage guys involved in individualized, high-endurance or weight-classified sports are at a higher risk for developing eating disorders. They'll engage in either bingeing and purging to cut weight, fasting to lose weight, or bingeing to put on more weight ("bulk up"). In the process, many guys get sucked into the Adonis Complex and experience muscle dysmorphia. And many more teenage guys fall victim to eating disorders because they have poor self-esteem, feel depressed, use eating as a coping mechanism, and a host of other psychological issues.

1.9 EFFECTS OF EATING DISORDERS

Eating disorders are treatable. But as I mentioned earlier, the treatment is as complex as the disorder. Although it's a time-intensive process, someone with an eating disorder can be whole again. However, if an eating disorder isn't attended to, or if the disordered teen doesn't heed the treatment plan, it can result in a number of physiological problems.

BONE AND MUSCLE GROWTH

An eating disorder not only weakens the bones and muscles, but it can also affect their development. Eating disorders can deplete the body of certain hormones essential to normal healthy growth. A preteen or early teen with an eating disorder can run the risk of impeding his or her physiological growth.

CARDIOVASCULAR DISEASE

This condition may start with high blood pressure and cholesterol. The teen can also develop an abnormal glucose tolerance. Dramatic weight loss can affect the enrichment of the blood, which may result in anemia and a weakened immune system. When a person loses a lot of weight, there's a depletion of stored body fat. So the body responds by breaking down the muscles, including the heart muscle. Conversely, when someone gains a lot of weight, the heart is strained by having to work harder. Thus, the continuous rise and decline in a person's weight can profoundly weaken the heart and lead to results ranging from poor circulation to a higher risk of heart attack.

MALNUTRITION

While it's easy to believe that an anorexic teen runs the risk of being malnourished, those suffering with bulimia and even binge-eating disorder can also experience malnutrition despite maintaining a stable weight or even gaining weight. Nutrients are absorbed into the system of a person who binges (and purges), yet malnutrition can still occur depending on the content of what's being eaten.

One of the major signs of malnutrition is a shift in the body's normal metabolism. Thyroid hormone production changes as a natural protective mechanism, reducing the body's caloric requirements. In effect, the body is saving the good nutrition while garbage is still being dumped into the teen's system. Body temperature, blood enrichment, heart function, and blood pressure are all affected when metabolism shifts because they require a higher caloric count to function at their premium.

As malnourishment continues, the size and function of various internal organs is affected. The brain, kidneys, reproductive organs, and heart can decrease in mass, thereby compromising their functioning. In addition, other organs, like the liver, may increase in fatty content, which compromises its function. Bone density also becomes compromised leading to weakened bones and joint pain. Other signs of malnutrition can also be seen: Hair loss, brittle nails, feeling cold all the time, headaches, dizziness or blacking out, skin problems, constant fatigue, jaundice, constipation or other bowel problems, as well as loss of menstruation in girls and decreased sexual libido in guys.

DAMAGE TO THE DIGESTIVE SYSTEM

Purging by induced vomiting can be destructive to the entire digestive tract. The mouth and esophagus become overexposed to stomach acid, which can create ulcers, erode dental enamel, and burn the lining of the affected areas. The retching from induced vomiting can produce tearing in the stomach lining and esophagus. Salivary glands will also become inflamed because of the increased production of saliva to accommodate the trauma to the mouth and throat. This swelling can make the jaw, throat, and even cheeks look puffy.

The digestive system can also be further compromised by the use of diuretics and laxatives. The loss of fluids from the perpetual use of these products compromises the function of the bowels. The user may start having diarrhea but then become constipated, thereby increasing the need for laxatives and putting the affected teen in a dangerous cycle. Diuretics and laxatives also result in a loss of fluids and electrolytes, or dehydration, which we'll discuss next.

DEHYDRATION

Electrolytes are substances (such as potassium, sodium, chloride, and bicarbonate) in the body that regulate the proper flow of the body's normal electrical current and are activated in the body's fluids. The balance of electrolytes is therefore essential for normal cell and organ function. Dehydration (or the loss of electrolytes), resulting from either purging or a lack of proper nutrition, can lead to muscle cramping, seizures, and ultimately heart arrhythmia or failure.

Lack of thirst isn't the only possible indicator that an individual is dehydrated. Medical professionals say the best barometer is the color of one's urine. If urine is clear and slightly yellow, then hydration is good. If it's dark yellow to amber in color, then it's showing signs of dehydration.

The symptoms of dehydration can include dry mouth, fatigue or sleepiness, muscle weakness, decreased urine output, sunken eyes, low blood pressure, rapid heartbeat, dizziness, or delirium. When left untreated, dehydration can lead to heart failure, cerebral edema (swelling of the brain), seizures, kidney failure, drop in blood pressure, hypovolemic shock (a lack of oxygenated blood enriching the body tissues), coma, and death.

DEATH

Eating disorders are deadly. As you can see from the vast list of possible harmful effects from a lack of proper nutrition, as well as an understanding of the body's need and function regarding strenuous exercise, any abuse of those two things can result in death. It's ignorant to believe that death is always a slow process with an eating disorder. The damage done to an affected teen's system can weaken the heart, and any physical or emotional stress can result in a sudden heart attack. Even while I was writing this book, the headlines in the news told of a teenage guy who fell over dead on the football field from over-exercise. An adolescent's outward appearance isn't always a good gauge for the internal damage that's being done by this deadly disorder.

1.10 ACCOMPANYING PSYCHOLOGICAL PROBLEMS

Earlier in this book, I stated that eating disorders have comorbidity with other issues, problems, or disorders. *Comorbidity* means there is an additional problem that's occurring simultaneously. Often one issue feeds off or plays into the other. This is why treatment for an eating disorder can be complex and time intensive. It's important that people who live or work with teenagers are aware of the issues that have comorbidity.

ESTEEM ISSUES

People with eating disorders often have low self-esteem issues. They tend to see themselves as less valuable or less important than others. People who have low self-esteem define themselves by their faults, failures, flaws, inabilities, and weaknesses, or by what they are not or don't have. Teens with low self-esteem engage in constant negative and critical self-talk. These messages are so ingrained in their hearts and minds that it often takes intense therapy to help the teens accurately assess themselves and reframe their thinking.

OBSESSIVE COMPULSIVE DISORDER

This is the recurrence of unwanted thoughts or images and uncontrolled behaviors. Often these all-consuming thoughts or obsessions and uncontrolled ritualistic behaviors or compulsions are so pervasive that they alter the individual's lifestyle, normal routines, relationships, and ability to cope. Someone with an obsessive-compulsive disorder often lives with high levels of anxiety, fear, and dread.

MOOD DISORDERS

Teens with eating disorders may also experience a major depressive disorder, anxiety disorder, or bipolar disorder.

- Major depression is a persistent, overwhelming feeling of sadness, loss, or defeat that impairs the quality of life, as well as normal life functions. Major depression can lead to suicide ideations and attempts.
- Anxiety disorder is when a teen feels persistent, overwhelming stress over daily routines and decisions. Anxiety can also be accompanied by fear, panic, and dread. Many times this disorder leads to a disabling, immobilizing life.
- Bipolar disorder is a cyclical depression in which the teen fluctuates between manic (high) episodes and depressive (low) episodes. The manic episodes can be marked by irrational judgment and risk-taking to bouts of anger and rage. The depressive episodes can be disabling and lead to suicide ideation, contemplation, and attempts. (You can find more information about this issue in another book in this series entitled *What Do I Do When Teenagers are Depressed and Contemplate Suicide?*)

INAPPROPRIATE COPING SKILLS

Coping skills refer to the thought processes and set of behaviors used to effectively deal with negative life circumstances. Coping skills help us navigate life's tragedies and traumas, relational conflicts, and stressful or painful situations. A positive coping skill may be seeking advice from informed people, whereas a negative coping skill would be ignoring a problem. For many teens with eating disorders, eating behaviors become a negative coping skill. In another way, having poor coping skills can make out-of-control eating habits worse. Teens learn positive coping behaviors by observing healthy family members and friends (modeling) and through the direct intervention (teaching) of caring adults.

SEXUAL ABUSE

Teens who've been sexually abused may also present with an eating disorder. Many times they hate their bodies or are so disgusted by the things that have happened to them that they'll try to drastically alter their bodies in an attempt to ward off the assaults. In some cases the eating disorder may develop during the time period in which the teens are still being abused. The idea behind this response is that if the abused teenagers become repulsively fat or skinny, then they'll no longer be desirable to their abusers.

SUBSTANCE ABUSE

Some teens with eating disorders start smoking cigarettes. The smoking becomes a literal smoke screen to mask other inappropriate behaviors like bingeing and purging. Inducing vomiting makes the teen's breath smell of vomit, but the smoking hides these odors. It's often easier for teens to battle with their parents over smoking than to have their eating disorder discovered. Parents are less likely to seek treatment over a smoking habit than an eating disorder.

Some teens don't limit their bingeing to only foods. They may often resort to alcohol bingeing as well. This is a dangerous behavior because alcohol can be rapidly absorbed into the teen's system. While they may vomit up the liquid, they're not ridding themselves of the ingested alcohol.

1.11 FAMILY STRESS

It's important to start this section by saying that not all eating disorders have roots in family dysfunction and that not all dysfunctional families experience eating disorders. That means someone from a great family can still develop an eating disorder. While families may or may not be a direct variable in the formation of the eating disorder, they're essential to the healing and wholeness of the suffering teenager.

Many families feel hesitant or threatened when they're asked to take part in the therapeutic intervention of their struggling teenager. They afraid they've created the problem and that weaknesses and dysfunction in their parenting will be pointed out during the process. Parents must work past their fears and realize that their family is the primary and most dominant defining context on the teenager's life. Effective help for a struggling teen includes family involvement in the therapeutic intervention.

A family's ideologies, values, idiosyncrasies, and behaviors are imprinted on a child and may become more exaggerated in adolescence. A family may be unaware that their actions and words may lead their teen toward unhealthy thinking and behaviors. However, words are powerful and can have a positive or negative effect on the identity of a child. Here are some examples:

- Parents who make self-abasing comments like, "I'm so fat and ugly," can lead their children to believe the parents are making the same judgments about them.
- Parents who inappropriately comment about their children's weight ("You'd better not eat so many sweets. You don't want to get fat," or "Boys don't ask out chunky girls," or "Girls don't

like fat boys") can germinate fears and a pervasive feeling that they're not acceptable the way they are.

- Many times teens who experience verbal abuse in their families will resort to eating as a means of comfort or rebellion. Targeting a teen's physical appearance during a fit of anger is an example of the type of verbal abuse that may precipitate an eating problem. (For instance, saying something like, "Clean your room—I'm tired of you being such a lazy lard@#$.")

- Even affectionate pet names for children (for example, "chubby bunny," and so on) may wreak havoc in the children's psyche when they reach their teenage years. A&E aired an episode of *Intervention* that was about twin girls named Sonia and Julia who were admitted into a program for severe eating disorders. They came to discover that as the twins were growing up, the family often referred to Julia as the "bigger twin" because she developed earlier. This was done in an affectionate and descriptive way just because she was three inches taller and fuller (but in no way fatter) than her sister. Friends would hear the family do this, and they'd also tease Julia about being the bigger twin. Thus, in her teenage years, Julia began a rebellious campaign of not being the bigger twin. In response, Sonia became fearful of now being the bigger of the two girls, so she also began eating destructively, too. Both girls became codependent and enmeshed in fear and a destructive cycle of behaviors.[23]

Families can also pass on bad habits and behaviors to their children. Coping skills are usually learned through observation. Parents who resort to eating or drinking as a way of overcoming stress will model this for their children. As teens approach a stressful time in their lives, they begin mimicking these learned coping skills. Eating for comfort can turn into a reliance on food. As teens come to understand this—usually because they start to put on weight—they may then go in the opposite direction and develop a rebellion against food, resulting in their starvation.

Some parents live vicariously through their children. Dreams of seeing their daughter become a prima ballerina or their son a medal-winning gymnast can become overbearing. These parents may push their kids to achieve while believing that their dreams are also their teens' dreams. This close scrutiny extends into the teens' eating and exercise habits. The high expectations and demands of a parent can lead teens to eat (or not eat) as a form of rebellion or a means to be in control.

Remuda Ranch is a residential treatment center focused on helping people with eating disorders, and they've identified some additional characteristics of the families they encounter in treatment.[24] This isn't a comprehensive list, but it can offer further insight into the family dynamics of affected teens:

- Distant fathers
- Chaotic families or families with substance abuse problems
- A mother with high expectations for her daughter
- Demanding parents
- Parents who openly foster sibling rivalries
- Over-controlling or domineering parents
- A father's depression, rigidity, or excessive self-discipline
- Marital conflict
- Parents' sexual relationship problems
- High levels of parent-daughter stress and family tension
- Fathers who are chronically ill
- Family members who are disconnected from their own feelings and who become emotionally distant from others

Understanding How Theology Informs Eating, Exercise, and Body Issues

| Section 2 |

2.1 BASIC THEOLOGICAL STARTING POINTS

A friend recently asked me, "Does our theology really address the issue of eating disorders?" He was implying that Scripture and theology don't really approach this particular issue and that trying to connect the two would be a stretch.

I replied, "I think that as followers of Jesus we should approach every value that we hold to, every conviction that we follow, every action that we take or do not take, every conversation, thought, and desire through the grid of 'Christ.' So our theology should mandate that we understand and act as advocates for hurting teens."

I was trying to encourage him that youth ministry should be concerned with the plights of adolescents around the world. We should bring hope, healing, and light into sick and dark places.

So I asked my friend, "Why aren't youth ministries leading the charge against this disorder that's literally taking the lives of countless teenagers all around the globe?" He was challenged to rethink and reframe his theology on the issue.

2.1A A VIEW FROM CHURCH HISTORY

Eating disorders aren't new to the church. As a matter of fact, starvation was once practiced as a form of holiness. Many holy women of the medieval era engaged in a "holy anorexia."[25] They believed the body was a carnal expression of sexuality and sin. Out of a desire for piety and in an attempt to be chaste, women altered the shape of their bodies by not eating, and men ate very little in order to keep themselves from loving pleasure and being self-indulgent. Their belief was that the sacrament of communion should be their truest source of sustenance.

It's believed that Saint Teresa of Ávila would induce vomiting with twigs from an olive tree so she would be rid of any impurity that would interfere with the sustenance she could receive from the communion Host.[26] Denying oneself of food, sleep, conversation, and giving oneself over to personal (sometimes self-inflicted) suffering was thought to be a way for a person to achieve holiness.

In one study of 170 Italian medieval saints, it was found that over half of them suffered from this "holy anorexia."[27] At age 15, Saint Catherine of Siena began a fast to denounce her corporeality or her attachments to her physical body. She was under duress because her parents were arranging her marriage, but she wanted to remain chaste as a vow of her holiness. She lost half her body weight before a local priest ordered her to eat. She was torn between being obedient to the priest and keeping her vow to renounce her dependence on food. So she resorted to vomiting to keep her vow. After two years, her father finally gave up his plans to have her married. Catherine emerged to take a vow of chastity, and her ensuing ministry was marked by prayer and attention to the sick. She continued to live a lifestyle of self-starvation, always attempting to rid herself of any food that might stay in her stomach. Like many others, she induced vomiting as an act of purging, labeling it an act of justice for the miserable sin she committed.[28]

The Catholic Church regarded Saint Catherine as a great woman of God and a strong influential voice during a very dark era in the church's history. She was canonized as a saint and ranked among the Doctors of the Church—a title given only to those who've shaped Catholic Church doctrine. Faithful to her vows, Saint Catherine died at the age of 33 from holy anorexia. This type is different from what we see today because it grows out of a pilgrimage of holiness and self-denial. Many people were willing to lose their lives to starvation if they believed that food kept them from a deeper connection to Christ. In the eras following the medieval period, thinness continued to be viewed as a sign of spirituality because a person was considered to be disciplined enough to abstain from the sinful pleasures of gluttony.

The church's perspective on food throughout history has been peculiar, to say the least. There were times when it was believed that the consumption of food should be guarded and minimal because demons could enter the body while a person was eating. There have been times when the church believed that spices and spicy foods could lead to sexual immorality. Some people even engaged in self-mutilation and painful exercises to buffet their bodies into a perfection of holiness. The most common form of self-denial that grew out of the ascetic practices of Christian monasticism was fasting. However fasting back then and fasting today are two very different things. Saint Catherine and Saint Teresa practiced a lifestyle of fasting, which ultimately led to the willful yielding of their lives for holiness. Today we don't view this spiritual discipline as a continuing lifestyle of depriving oneself of food. We'll discuss fasting in more detail later on in this section.

2.1B FORGIVENESS AND REDEMPTION

As with many other issues we've covered in this What Do I Do When... series, the starting point for helping those who are afflicted with eating disorders is the expression of unconditional love and value. Teens who struggle with eating disorders believe they're worthless. Their eating problems are an attempt to feel valuable.

We can also expect that many teens experience resulting spiritual difficulties. They may feel—

- Out of touch with God
- Unworthy of God's love
- A sense of inadequacy or not measuring up
- As though God is judging or condemning them
- That they have deeply disappointed God
- Tremendous shame and guilt[29]

We need to cultivate a strong theology of forgiveness and redemption for teens who struggle with this issue. Struggling teens believe they're outside the realm of forgiveness. They believe their years of struggle and addictive behaviors have made God tired of their sinfulness, so God will no longer extend grace to them.

Adults need to teach and live out that redemption is not just a single act or event but an ongoing process. We are redeemed moment by moment. This also needs to be expressed in our churches by striving to be a much more gracious community. Teens hear us teach this, but then they observe us being ungracious and unforgiving as a church. We fail to wrestle through how this theological truth is worked out in our daily living. We become so afraid that our acts of grace and forgiveness will be seen as compromise.

Recently I was reading the work of a prominent Christian author who railed against the church for compromising because we restore fallen Christian leaders and pastors back to their positions. His premise was that their sins disqualify them from ministry. He viewed the church as being tolerant of sin and disregarding the biblical mandate that those in positions of leadership are charged with a higher standard. I believe this rigid perspective is damaging to others—especially those who are struggling. It keeps people at arm's length, trapped in the false belief that they're outside the grace of God. Instead, we need to be a gracious, loving, forgiving, and redemptive community that marks us as Christ's church.

We must never forget that as the body of Christ, the church, love is our defining mark. That love brings healing into the lives of hurting people. The power of God lies in a God-infused love that he pours through us. Love covers sin. Loves heals brokenness. Love unites hearts.

What hurting teens need most is to experience the love of God. They must know that their lives are so precious and valuable to God that he was willing to trade the life of his Son for theirs. As youth leaders, we need to share with teens that they can find unconditional acceptance in Christ. God loves them with an eternal, immeasurable, full, and rich love. They need to know they don't have to earn God's love and acceptance. They *can't* earn it. God offers it to us for free.

To communicate this amazing love, we must embody it. That means letting go of attitudes and desires of condemnation and judgment, while embracing the truth that Jesus paid it ALL. We must embrace a kingdom agenda of love, allowing God to lavish his love on us and through us.

2.1C CONTROL

Control is a deep-seated issue for teenagers who are engaged in an eating disorder. They believe their circumstances are out of their control, so in an attempt to regain control, they control their sustenance intake and output. As a result, the physiological and psychological effects (empowerment, endorphin rush, sense of accomplishment, and so on) give the teenager a sense of security and being in control.

A Christian teenager needs to make a complex theological shift and relinquish their control to God. This isn't an easy process, nor is it quick. And let's be perfectly honest here, you don't have to suffer from an eating disorder to experience difficulties allowing God to be in control of your life. We all worry about losing our jobs, keeping relationships, getting through crises, and the list goes on. So this is an "every-Christian" struggle.

This is probably a good place to insert a disclaimer: Confronting teens about trusting God will only make them more resistant. Telling adolescents they just need to trust God more is like slapping a few Bible-verse Band-Aids on a complex issue, which only makes you look ignorant and will most likely result in a loss of credibility with that teen.

Be mindful of the fact that a lack of nourishment can affect the physiology of the brain, resulting in a hypersensitivity that makes the individual power up and fight to stay in control. Teens with an eating disorder need to relearn to trust God and give over their control to him. Relinquishing any form of control means risking vulnerability. It's incredibly frightening for them. Fear clouds their judgment and causes them to put on blinders. Thus, they can't see that they aren't fat—even though they weigh only 98 pounds. When people try to reach out and show they care, these teens really believe they're actually part of a conspiracy to destroy them by making them fat and ugly.

This trust issue becomes more complex as teens begin to feel helpless and hopeless about their situations. They already believe their efforts to be loved and accepted are hopeless, so they determine to eat less as a means of regaining some personal power. The cycle becomes endless and exhausting. And a deeper hopelessness sets in as teens believe they aren't worth rescuing.

Adults should help teenagers understand that everyone within the body of Christ must sincerely trust in God for everything day by day. Adolescents' struggles may be different, but they're just as difficult as ours—and seemingly hopeless. We also need to model how we daily place our trust in God. Modeling this will take us off a spiritual pedestal and put us on equal footing with hurting teens. It also demonstrates the theological truth that the body of Christ is a community that hurts together and trusts God together. Doing this can be a real challenge within our culture, because the church in America is marked with an attitude of self-sufficiency. We trust what we *know* about God more than we actually trust God (things unseen). We've built our practices on the philosophy that "God helps those who help themselves," even believing this is biblical. We've become so accustomed to trusting in our belief systems and structures that we fail to see that we aren't trusting God at all.

So, in order to really help teens surrender control of their lives to God, we must model it first. We begin by asking God to make us aware of the areas of our lives in which we aren't giving God control. This astute awareness should lead to an honesty that allows a struggling teen to undertake a journey of trust alongside of us.

Matthew 6:25-27 is a great passage to help us consider our perspective on life and faith.

> Jesus says, "Therefore I tell you, do not worry about your life, what you will eat or drink; or about your body, what you will wear. Is not life more important than food, and the body more important than clothes? Look at the birds of the air; they do not sow or reap or store away in barns, and yet your heavenly Father feeds them. Are you not much more valuable than they? Can any one of you by worrying add a single hour to your life?"

Preceding this verse, Jesus talks to his disciples about finances, dreams of security, and future hopes. He then asks his followers to trust. Though focused on different issues from those of a struggling teen, we must realize our own tendencies to worry. Worry stems from a desire to be in control. This realization is the beginning of our trust walk with the Savior. If we want teens to know that Jesus can break the bondage of their eating issues, then we must allow Jesus to free us in those areas in which we're similarly bound.

Here are a few questions that will help you integrate this theological truth into your life:

- What do you fear?
- Identify a time when you felt out of control. What was that about?
- What do you worry about?
- If God took everything away, could you, like Job, say, "Yet will I trust him"?
- Do you do things for the approval of others?
- Do you believe there are things you need to do in order to win God's favor or to stay in God's favor?

These questions will serve as a starting place for you to examine your own trust walk.

Remember, God hasn't given us a spirit of fear but one of power and love and self-discipline (2 Timothy 1:7). We need to pray the first step prayer of recovery before we can ask hurting teens to pray it:

Dear Lord,
I admit that I am powerless over my addiction. I admit that my life is unmanageable when I try to control it. Help me this day to understand the true meaning of powerlessness. Remove from me all denial of my addiction. Amen.[31]

2.1D OTHER THEOLOGICAL CONSIDERATIONS
Volumes have been written about theological issues that inform

our practice and thinking surrounding current cultural issues. It's up to you to begin gathering information and cultivating a deeper understanding of the theologies (or in some cases, competing theologies) that intersect contemporary issues.

When approaching the issue of eating disorders, here are some additional theological considerations that a youth worker must develop:

- **A theology of reconciliation and hope** This idea is developed more in other books in the What Do I Do When... series. Eating disorders seem to be a hopeless issue that destroys relationships and families.
- **A theology of suffering and pain** This notion is also developed more within other books in this series. Parents and affected teens may ask why they have to suffer or why God allows such pain to come into their lives. As a side note, many teens with eating disorders feel as though they're suffering at the hands of an abuser. Our theology of justice and deliverance may inform how we approach this situation.
- **A theology of healing** Parents and teens may want answers regarding God's healing power. They may want to know if and how God heals, as well as the theological implications of healing in the life of an eating-disordered teenager.
- **A theology of prayer and deliverance** Teens and their families may pray fervently for God's deliverance, only to be confused as to why their prayers seem to go un-answered.
- **A theology of community and acceptance** Many teens with an eating disorder don't feel accepted. They often believe their control over food will help them change in a way that will help them find acceptance.

2.2 QUESTIONS THAT DEMAND THEOLOGICAL CONSIDERATION

2.2A AREN'T EATING DISORDERS AN ISSUE OF GLUTTONY OR VANITY?

Scripture lists gluttony and vanity as sins, but an eating disorder is much more complex than just an issue of rebellion. Eating disorders are a result of a broken and sinful human condition. In other words, sin stained our human existence, nature, world—everything. As a result, there are direct and indirect consequences to sin. Viewing an eating disorder as sin is similar to viewing sickness as sin. Now I know there are some who would hold to a theological position that all sickness *is* the direct result of sin in one's life. But for the most part, we could come to some agreement that there are situations that are indirectly stained by sin entering the world.

If eating disorders were simply a sin issue, like gluttony and vanity, then we'd see quicker recoveries. But this complex issue is rooted in the depths of a deeper issue that demands a powerful Redeemer who reconciles ALL things. Jesus' salvation isn't just for individual sin; it covers the effects of sin on all things, including nature. His salvation isn't just for our eternity but to right the damage that sin brings to a once-perfect world. Jesus' salvation is also a process—he continues to save us. It's not just a single event or one point in time. It doesn't act as a magic eraser to rid us of the horrible things we don't like. It's an ongoing, day-by-day, moment-by-moment reconciliation.

Teens with eating disorders need to know that God, through his redemptive process, started a good work in them and he will faithfully complete it. They need to know that old things will and do pass away and that all things are constantly becoming new. Where there is direct sin in their lives, they do need to bring it before God. But they also need to know that their ongoing struggles never disqualify them. God's love and redemption isn't contingent upon what they do or don't do (see Romans 8).

Teens with eating disorders would get out of their horrible cycle if they could, but they often feel like they didn't choose this, nor do they choose to continue in it. Our response is to patiently and lovingly nurture, support, encourage, and usher them into the arms of a loving Redeemer. For many of you, this may be difficult to understand because the issue can seem so theologically cut-and-dry. My challenge is to prayerfully put yourself in a place where you can let the Holy Spirit teach you, guide you, and shape your convictions.

2.2B IS FASTING A DANGEROUS FORM OF SELF-STARVATION OR A POSITIVE SPIRITUAL DISCIPLINE?

Fasting is a spiritual discipline that's designed to help us keep our focus on God. Simply put, not eating leads to the pangs of hunger. Those hunger pangs can then become prompts to put us in God's presence or remind us to rely more heavily upon God. Fasting was and is used as a means to draw closer to God by honing our focus on him (a hunger and thirst for righteousness or putting ourselves in a position of temporarily denying ourselves of something to learn to humbly trust in the sufficiency of God). It's used as a reminder to bring issues to God or to prayerfully acknowledge that God is in control. It's often done as a means of intense focus on God when seeking an answer or before making a critical decision.

The Bible never indicates that fasting is used as a means of personal purification (detoxification) or dieting. Fasting is always linked to prayer. Fasting is a reminder or prompt to pray. So while it's not so much about starving the body, it is about the feeding and restoration of the soul through a constant prompt to be in God's presence. So fasting becomes the temporary restriction of food and drink to accomplish drawing closer to God.

In Matthew 6:16-18, Jesus warns us to check the motives for our fasting.

"When you fast, do not look somber as the hypocrites do, for they disfigure their faces to show others they are fasting. Truly I tell you, they have received their reward in full. But when you fast, put oil on your head and wash your face, so that it will not be obvious to others that you are fasting, but only to your Father, who is unseen; and your Father, who sees what is done in secret, will reward you."

Jesus tells us fasting shouldn't be done out of impure motives or for personal gain. So we shouldn't have a dual purpose for fasting, such as drawing closer to God *and* losing weight. Fasting can be done for certain health benefits, but then it should be done with motives other than fasting for spiritual benefit.

People who suffer from eating disorders should not fast. Fasting is an activity that enables the eating disorder. Therefore, it can't be used as a means of drawing closer to God because of the baggage and link that it has to the disorder. We need to remember there is nothing sacred about spiritual disciplines in and of themselves. They're only methods, actions, and activities that assist us on a spiritual journey. A strong adherence or dependence on a spiritual discipline to bring a person into a right relationship with God is legalism. Teens who suffer from an eating disorder often believe they can fall out of God's grace by not fasting, or they use fasting as a spiritual smoke screen to justify their eating problem (the holy anorexia syndrome). Spiritual disciplines aren't designed to rob the physical life from the individual. It's only Satan who is out to murder and destroy the believer (1 Peter 5:8).

There are other spiritual disciplines that can help us accomplish the same results as fasting. Youth workers need to help teens find and develop disciplines that enhance their spiritual health and don't hinder their physical health. In addition, a fast doesn't have to be a temporary abstaining from food. It can also be done with other things the teen desires. Suggest they try fasting from their cell phones for a week. Every time they wish to call or text someone, they should use that as their prompt to pray. Or they could fast from the television. The time taken away from whatever activity they choose should be humbly spent in God's presence instead. Spiritual disciplines aren't holy and sacred; people can invent their own. However, spiritual disciplines are designed to keep us focused on God.

2.3 SCRIPTURE PASSAGES TO CONSIDER

Here are some Scripture passages that may prompt your thinking in developing a theological framework that informs this very complex issue. These passages aren't meant to be used as ammunition against teens. They're listed to give you a spiritual springboard into further theological thought.

- 1 Samuel 16:7—Helps us line up our values with God's values—both for ourselves and for others.
- Psalm 23:4; 27:1-3; 34:3-4; 46:1-3; Proverbs 3:24-26—Many teens who fall victim to eating disorders experience overwhelming fear. These passages help us identify where fear comes from and how to approach it.
- Psalm 139:14—A reminder that God values every part of our being, even our bodies.
- Proverbs 12:18—Words are powerful. Many teens engage in an eating disorder because they choose to believe negative words about their image, shape, or size. God gives us insight on the healing power of wise words.
- Proverbs 31:30—This verse can be used in harmful ways. Teenage girls need to understand the truth that their primary impact in others' lives won't be through their looks but through their relationship with God.
- 1 Corinthians 6:19-20—Offers insight into a sacred space. It's often used to guilt teens into changing their ways or as ammunition against eating disorders.
- 1 Corinthians 12:26-27—Gives us a different perspective on our role in the lives of those who suffer.
- James 1—Reminds us of the dangers of status and how we should or shouldn't treat others.
- 1 Peter 4:8—This verse, among many, describes the primary approach we should take with a teen who's struggling with any issue.

Practical Tips and Action to Take When Helping Teenagers Who Struggle With Eating Disorders

| Section 3 |

3.1 GIVING SUPPORT TO STRUGGLING TEENS

There are many preventative and remedial actions you can take to help teenagers who may be struggling with an eating disorder. The preventative actions listed below may keep kids from falling into destructive behaviors and thinking.

Eating disorders are not a confidential issue. This means that if a teen discloses to you that he or she is struggling with an eating problem, it isn't something you should keep confidential. You need to mobilize resources and get help for the teen. Instruct others who work with teenagers not to be put in a compromising position by agreeing to keep something secret before they find out what the secret is. If you believe that harm is being done to a minor, even if it's self-inflicted, you have a duty to warn.

Now, as a point of clarity, there is no statute that states you are mandated to report eating disorders. However, you could have a civil suit brought against you under tort laws that make you responsible for the knowledge you have if harm comes to the teen and you never acted responsibly on that knowledge. (More information on duty to warn laws and mandated reporting is explained in another book from this series: *What Do I Do When Teenagers Encounter Bullying and Violence?*)

Eating disorders aren't behaviors that should be kept in the confidence of a relationship. Inform teens that if their friends are talking about eating disorders or throwing up, they should inform a qualified adult. Many teens feel as though they're put in the middle because their friends ask them not to disclose their eating problems. Empower teens to get help for their friends. Openly talking to a youth group about this issue and giving teens an action plan that empowers them to help gives them a standard of behavior that protects them from being labeled as untrustworthy.

Educate yourself and others about eating disorders. Make sure parents, other youth workers, and even the teens in your youth ministry know the facts about eating disorders. Remember, these are deadly disorders and the myths and ignorance surrounding this issue can compromise a teenager's life.

Know *when* to refer. This complex issue demands the attention of professionals who have expertise with eating disorders and obsessive-compulsive disorders. While you do assist in the healing of these teens by being in a supportive role, you aren't equipped to be in a position of oversight or primary care. Too many youth workers have messiah complexes in which they believe they can rescue kids from their brokenness (in the name of Jesus, of course). In truth, I applaud the passion that keeps youth workers on the frontlines and knee-deep in adolescents' emotional baggage. That kind of love is amazing, but it mustn't be clouded by a need to be needed. Recognize that you aren't the kind of professional that's needed in this situation. And just because you read this book or know a lot about eating disorders or have experienced an eating disorder yourself, that still doesn't qualify you. **So at the onset of your discovery that a teen is struggling with an eating disorder—refer, refer, refer.**

Know *how* **to refer.** Every youth ministry should have a list of area counselors, clinics, or medical practices that specialize in adolescent issues. If you don't have one, now would be a good time to establish this referral base before you find yourself in the middle of a crisis. And it's important that you include people who have expertise with eating disorders. Then make that list available to parents. Inform parents of the specific behaviors, conversations, and attitudes you've observed in their teens. Suggest that they have a qualified mental or medical health professional evaluate the situation. Do this in the name of a better-safe-than-sorry rule.

Here are some places to begin as you start forming your referral base:

- Contact therapists and clinics in your area. Tell them you're building a referral base for teens and families who are struggling. Makes sure they have expertise with adolescent disorders and, in this case, eating disorders. It's not out of bounds for you to interview individual therapists and ask questions about their openness to offer spiritual support in the therapeutic intervention or any other questions you may have. If there are mental health professionals in your congregation, start there. However, there may be some boundary issues to consider first. A family may feel uncomfortable seeing a therapist whom they also see in social and spiritual contexts. But therapists in your congregation can also recommend other qualified therapists.

- Contact the nearest hospital and arrange to talk with someone in their psychiatric department. Every hospital has a psychiatrist on staff.
- Network with larger churches that have access to counseling facilities and mental health professionals. Some larger churches also have professional counselors on staff or have access to them through their congregation.
- Contact the nearest Christian university's psychology department. They may have alumni or know of a qualified professional in your area with whom you can network.

Require that every teen attend all meals during retreats, camps, or mission trips. Use meal times as a time of announcement or assessment. That means everyone needs to attend and stay there until they're dismissed. Students may complain they don't like the food or they're not hungry. But help them to see that this is family time—everyone's presence is required, whether or not they eat. Let them know they aren't required to eat; they're just required to be there through the duration of the meal. This will keep your teens accountable, help to create a more socially cohesive group, and also give you insight into the eating patterns of the teens you're concerned about.

Be careful not to spotlight "beautiful" teens or promote only those teens as leaders. There is an antiquated youth ministry philosophy that touted, "If you win the athletes and cheerleaders at a school, you can win the school." This view plays into warped societal views of importance and teenage insecurities about popularity, body image, and looks. While most ministries will never verbalize this value, many adhere to it by their actions. If only the popular, beautiful kids are in visible positions—positions of service or leadership—then you're sending a loud-and-clear message. Many congregations also hold to this value in their adult and children's ministries. Help bring to light how this approach to ministry is damaging and shapes the values teens internalize.

I was in a conversation with a group of church leaders who were discussing how they screen those people who'll be up front during their services. They were describing the specific ways people must look in order to be on the stage. These leaders believed that overweight people were embarrassing to the church and might hinder people from worshipping there. They saw overweight as a sin of gluttony and made that comparable to having an adulterer leading the worship time. WHAT?! They also selected the apparel to be worn by all upfront personnel using photographs of these people's wardrobes. All of this was in the name of excellence in ministry. Some churches select their greeters and ushers using similar criteria.

Do you think Jesus chose only the thin, beautiful, and talented people to be his disciples? Our teens need to see that *all* are welcomed, significant, have something to contribute, and belong in the body of Christ. I'm familiar with a very dynamic youth ministry that, according to its youth pastor, is completely made up of the community's misfits, losers, and unpopular students. You'll see teens who don't fit society's mold of "beautiful" serving others, but they're the most beautiful youths on the face of the planet. The interesting thing is that this ministry is reaching and helping severely hurting teens find wholeness in Christ. I think a youth group like that gives us a glimpse of heaven.

Openly challenge societal views, as well as your youth group's collective priorities, values, and attitudes about beauty and status. Help teenagers see the shallowness of being defined by looks, body type and image, and the clothing one wears. God looks at our hearts—not how cut or curvy we are. Help them adopt this same value. Help students recognize and discern the messages they're bombarded with every day.

Consider the following research cited by the National Eating Disorders Association:[31]

- A study of 4,294 network television commercials revealed that 1 out of every 3.8 commercials send some sort of "attractiveness message," telling viewers what is or is not attractive. These researchers estimate that the average adolescent sees more than 5,260 "attractiveness messages" a year.
- A study of one teen adolescent magazine over the course of 20 years found that in articles about fitness or exercise plans, 74 percent cited "to become more attractive" as a reason to start exercising, and 51 percent noted the need to lose weight or burn calories.
- Another study of mass media magazines discovered that women's magazines had 10.5 times more advertisements and articles promoting weight loss than men's magazines did, and that 60 percent of Caucasian middle-school girls read at least one fashion magazine regularly.
- The average American woman is 5'4" tall and weighs 140 pounds. The average American model is 5'11" tall and weighs 117 pounds. Most fashion models are thinner and taller than 98 percent of all American women.[32]
- During childhood and adolescence, media exposure is part of a constellation of sociocultural factors that promote a thinness schema for girls and the muscularity schema for boys.[33]

Teach teens to respect themselves and others. God created diversity in body types. Lack of acceptance based on how a person looks is prejudice. Remind them that physical appearance has nothing to do with, nor does it define, the quality, character, and value of a person. Help them to adopt a personal "no tolerance" policy against those who tease someone because of their weight, size, shape, or looks.

Inform teens about the dangers of altering their bodies without the supervision of a qualified medical professional or an informed adult. Youth workers do more in a student's life than just discipleship. We also teach and model life skills. So encourage teens to exercise for fun and health and to eat a healthy, balanced diet. Be the voice of reason in the ears of guys who start to weight train obsessively. Many guys start lifting prematurely in their development and become obsessed because they don't see the changes they desire. Be the voice of reason in the ears of girls who believe they should strive to be thinner. Keep your radar up for any talk about dieting, losing weight, or even joking about eating disorders. Don't argue that they aren't fat or don't need to diet. Instead, challenge them to do it right by having someone qualified coach them. This makes the teen accountable. Then model the above behaviors in your own life.

Monitor a coach's behavior and generate public concern, if needed. Don't overlook or dismiss conversations when teens are dropping weight for a sport at a coach's suggestion. Realize that the "suggestions" of a coach are often as law-leveling as a mandate. Teens are often fearful of being cut from a sport, not played, or intentionally overlooked if they don't follow the coach's suggestions. Many coaches use such tactics to control an athlete's behavior. If a coach is more concerned with his or her win-loss record over the well-being of the athlete, then this is dangerous.

By the way, I've never met a coach who verbally claims their record is more important than the athlete. Rather, I've heard many athletes say that coaches don't care about them, won't listen to them or be understanding of their life situations, and so on. This should give you reason to stand as an advocate for the student athletes in your community. If the school board pressures and solely evaluates a coach based on his or her record, then petition the board. Conversely, champion those coaches who become concerned when athletes engage in eating and exercise patterns that are destructive, who are more concerned about the total development of their athletes (especially their character) than winning, or who become advocates for struggling athletes.

Openly confront times when media makes light of eating disorders. Call it out to parents and teens. There's been a series of teen comedies that display popular, beautiful teens in a sarcastic light and portray bingeing or vomiting behaviors as normative. Media can sometimes make eating disorders look easy, normative, and glamorous, even when it's poking fun. Those movies and programs present opportunities for "teachable moments."

Listen. Teens who struggle with eating disorders often have trust issues. They don't want their behaviors to be discovered, so they hide and are often suspicious of everyone. If teens are willing to talk with you about their struggles, then listen to them. Be slow to speak. Don't let your desire to help become so urgent that it gets in the way of your listening. Hear the teens enough to empathize with their pain. Listen with the intent of understanding the complexities and desperation that led these teens into destructive eating patterns. Be sure you're asking more questions than offering solutions and advice. Ask open-ended questions—ones that don't require a single-word (yes or no) answer. When you listen, give teens your undivided attention. This is a great demonstration of love and value. Also listen with empathetic ears. Let teens talk about whatever they're feeling.

Help struggling teens focus on character quality. Teens must be made aware of and taught to understand several things:

- What it means to be a child of God
- That the true measure of a person is character—not looks, abilities, or skills
- That God loves and accepts us—and nothing can interfere or separate us from God's love
- That people who love God also love and accept the things God loves—namely precious teens
- That God measures us by our hearts, not our outward appearances
- That God instills great qualities and characteristics in each of us (in other words, love, wisdom, goodness, hope, patience, and so on)

Help teenagers cultivate those qualities, and then make sure you notice and applaud them when they display them. Also make a point of talking to teens more about whose they are than who they are. There is transforming power in an understanding that we are in God's ownership (God bought us at a great price) and that he gives us family rights as heirs with Christ. Teens need a strong sense of acceptance and belonging that must be centered in a continual knowledge of whose they are.

Help teens understand their physiological development. Teens know only theoretically or part of what's happening with their bodies. After they experience the physiological changes to their reproductive system, they forget that their bone and muscle mass is still changing. This can be seen even in pictures of a person between their freshman and senior years in college. And the growth maturation is still remarkably different and becomes even more complete at ages 22 or 23. When we help our teens realize that physiological changes are normal and occur throughout the life span of adolescence, it helps balance their feelings of abnormality.

Promote a positive self-esteem by emphasizing the value that each individual has in God's eyes. I was talking to a young guy who was struggling with his physical limitations. He was defining his worth by what he could or couldn't do physically and by his health and appearance. He said, "If I can't get stronger, then I'm just worthless." At first I thought he was making a passing comment out of frustration. But as I probed more, I became very aware that he believed his assessment to be true. I asked him if he knew how valuable he was. I prodded to see if he really knew his worth. I reminded him that he was so valuable that he cost the life of God's Son. Remind teens that God values us enough to give his life in payment for us.

Talk with teens about proper coping skills. Coping skills are the behaviors we move through to take us from feeling negative feelings like stress and pain to positive feelings. Many coping skills are modeled, so teens learn to just adapt them over the years as learned behaviors. A parent who curses and throws things in a fit of rage is modeling an inappropriate coping skill that the teen eventually emulates. Coping skills are also learned by trial and error. For example, a teen may have never witnessed someone eating to alleviate stress, but she can happen upon it by finding comfort in food during a stressful life episode. This behavior is then rein-forced and repeated during times of stress. Teens with eating and body image problems often resort to eating, purging, and abusing exercise as coping mechanisms. But any learned behavior can be unlearned and relearned. Encourage teens to learn some of the following new coping skills instead of resorting to eating:

- Engage in positive self-talk. Instead of continuing to focus on self-abasing thoughts, help them to repeat things like, "I'm a valuable child of the King of the Universe. That makes me royalty." This can also take on the form of visual remind-ers, where objects (bookmarks, cards, photos, and so on) are strategically placed as reminders for the teen. Memorizing Scripture can also help teens saturate their minds with God's Word—it's a powerful way to live and think Christian.

- Find a couple of trusted adults whom they can talk to when they're feeling stressed. Often talking about the negative feelings helps put them in perspective enough to make life more manageable. Talking is a powerful coping skill.

- Journal. Many times this can be a creative and productive coping mechanism. Teens can blog or journal their thoughts and feelings in a way that will help them get past the nega-tive feelings.

- Read. Sometimes this relaxation skill can help teens get out of the panic of the moment and allow them to relax enough so their perspective is redefined.

- Deep breathing. This can help teens relax and get a bit more centered. Breathing is often followed by exercise of some sort, releasing the endorphins that help relieve stress. But teens with eating disorders often make strenuous exercise a part of their obsessive behavior. In these cases, teens need to find other coping skills. Going for walks is a good activity to accompany deep breathing.

- Pet care. Taking responsibility for, playing with, and caring for an animal takes teenagers' minds off themselves. When teens have difficulty coping, suggest that they take the dog for a walk. This may sound lame, but surprisingly it works. There have been many breakthroughs in therapeutic situations when animals are brought into the picture. Individuals must re-engage and align their behaviors in a responsible, loving way—all directed at the pet.

- Serve. Help teens network with a social service organization where they can serve others regularly and in a variety of ways, from playing with children on a pediatric ward of a hospital to serving in a food pantry to helping the elderly in an assisted living situation. Once again this helps divert the teens' destructive self-centered notions and makes them more focused on others. Service is a powerful tool to help teens change their destructive behaviors. This is more effective when done as a regular appointment. Teens will begin to notice that there is less negativity and stress in their lives over the long haul.

- Be creative. Painting or drawing, singing, doing crafts or some other hobby can also become healthy coping skills. They help the teen relax, eliminate the stress of the moment, and allow them to return to the precipitating issue in a different state of mind. Some teens find dance to be a creative coping skill, but this may not be the right creative outlet for a teen with an eating disorder. The physical exercise of the dance can become a part of the abusive dysfunction that accompanies eating disorders.

- Prayer and worship. More than just coping skills, these become a source of strength and solution. Challenge teens to have times of personal worship as a part of their spiritual growth. The focus is then redirected toward God—who invites us to cast our cares on him. Encourage teens to pray prayers of thanksgiving (without asking for anything) and praise.

Challenge teens to find friends who don't focus on weight or outer appearance. Encourage them to be that kind of friend

as well. Like so many psychological disorders with teens, a shift in social circles often helps them overcome tough issues. If you're challenging your youth group to be a loving community, then it should be a place where teens aren't defined by their outward appearances. Yet many times this value is culturally and subconsciously ingrained. This is why support groups are necessary. You should encourage struggling teens to become involved in a support group. Many times this may be part of their therapy. As a loving helper in the life of hurting teens, you can encourage them to engage and contribute to their support group. Challenge them to be the type of friend they want others to be.

Helping a guy who has an eating disorder:

- Show him examples of men who are defined by godly character, not looks. Help him see that masculinity isn't defined by appearance.
- Help him understand that a real man isn't defined by power but by weaknesses that makes him depend on Jesus. Let him know and see that God is made strong in the life of a man who's weak.
- Help him understand that he isn't defined by what he does but by whose he is.
- Help him redefine success apart from his size, shape, appearance, and athleticism, by living out biblical values and trusting in Jesus.

3.2 CREATING A SAFE ENVIRONMENT

Teens who struggle with eating disorders often feel guilt and shame. Unfortunately, many have experienced the church's retribution and condemnation rather than consolation, reconciliation, and rehabilitation. Teens fear being humiliated and rejected. Teens will perceive the church as unsafe whenever they sense that only certain kinds of people are really accepted. A teen who is struggling will notice behaviors such as comments made about people who aren't the norm; who's given opportunities to lead, share, and be upfront at church; which people are engaged and attended to; and continual messages of division, fear of culture, and judgments that promote militant stands. When these behaviors are the mark of our churches, even if they're expressed in subtle ways, teens will be driven away. We need to ensure that our church and youth ministries are safe by fostering a loving community.

3.2A FOSTERING A LOVING COMMUNITY

Consider the attitude that you and your church staff have about weight and personal looks. If unattractive people are avoided or overlooked, invisible in the leadership structure, given little or no attention, or just tolerated, then you're creating an unsafe ministry environment. Challenge everyone in the church and your youth ministry to go out of their way to make sure everyone feels loved and accepted.

Make your youth group a place where teenagers are accepted. Verbalize this message of acceptance often. Help the teens in your ministry understand that people who are hurt, struggling, broken, or in need must be surrounded by positive, loving people. Together we bring God's healing into each other's lives.

Understand that you cannot talk *enough* about love being the defining mark of who we are. You should be a broken record—constantly repeating that we're going to be measured by our love and that we're only noise if we don't have love. Teach it, demonstrate it, allude to it in every message or talk, expect it to be the hallmark of the youth ministry's existence.

Educate teens so they have an awareness that they might contribute to someone else's eating problem whenever they:

- Make derogatory comments about someone's weight or make jokes about weight, looks, and body image
- Pay attention to or befriend only the beautiful people
- Consider a person's weight and looks to be important
- Compliment people for only their looks or performance (Many eating disordered teens have commented that they only received compliments after they lost weight. Teach teens to notice character qualities in action and compliment others for being patient, kind, loving, wise, or a good friend.)
- Fall victim to the media's presentation of a certain body type being the standard of beauty
- See beauty as only someone's physical appearance
- Make fun of someone's eating habits or choices (This should be particularly noted if someone who's thin has different habits. A recovering anorexic may have rituals surrounding the types of foods they eat and how. Poking fun at them draws attention to their dysfunction and can be misunderstood as condemnation.)
- Praise or glorify someone's appearance more than their character and internal qualities
- Fail to internalize God's values and standards of seeing someone as valuable because of who God made them to be, not for their outward appearance

3.2B HOW SHOULD I CONFRONT A TEEN WHO I BELIEVE IS STRUGGLING?

If you suspect that a teen has an eating disorder, you shouldn't ignore the situation. Here are some actions to take:

1. If possible, start by having a conversation with the teen's parent or guardian. Remember, parents may be a part of the problem. If you're unaware of the family dynamic or don't have a personal relationship with the parents, then you may not be able to judge whether or not parents will be a safe first line of help. For instance, a teenage girl may be engaged in an eating disorder because a family member is sexually abusing her. Going to the parent with your observations may only make the situation more volatile for the teen. If the family is loving and supportive and you have a relationship with them, talking with them should be your first line of action. By the way, if they're as loving and supportive as you perceive them to be, they may already have some concerns, which will only be validated by your observations. Make them aware of the behaviors, signs, and symptoms you're seeing. Then the confrontation of the teen may be better made with the parent present—or even by the parent—but in a very loving and supportive way.

2. Talk to the teen privately. Don't confront her in front of a friend—not even her best friend. For example, don't say, "I've noticed that you haven't been eating a lot lately," when you're with a group of teens at a restaurant. Confronting a teen about an eating disorder merits more planning and finesse than just finding an opportune moment. Make sure you're in a comfortable place and have plenty of time so there's no rush.

3. Make sure you're not judgmental. Express loving concern for the teen. Make sure the teen knows you don't think any less of her. On the contrary, tell her you highly value her and that's why you're so concerned about her. Teens fear they'll fall in your eyes.

4. Ask the teen to talk to a parent or guardian and suggest that she seek professional help. Don't let the teen talk to her parents alone, if at all possible. Arrange to be there in a supportive role. Help the teen rehearse what she'll say to her parents. If the teen believes she doesn't have a problem, encourage her to at least let a qualified professional make an assessment.

5. Don't let the teen manipulate you with denial, excuses, or justifications for her behaviors and eating patterns. Be straightforward about your concerns and observations. Verbalize the symptoms you see and the behaviors you've observed.

6. Be objective. State your observations, not your speculations. Express your concerns over the teen's health, attitudes, conversations, values, and behaviors—not just her appearance. Point out the behaviors you've seen (avoiding food, secretively disappearing during and after meals, relational withdrawal, and so on) and the conversation patterns that are obsessive regarding food and body awareness. Be specific in your examples. You may say, "Given those specific examples, I believe you could be struggling with an eating disorder."

7. If the teen becomes upset or angry during the confrontation, end the conversation by offering to resume talking another time. Share that you had some concerns you wanted to check out. Then keep an eye on the teen. If an eating disorder is present, more and more symptoms will manifest. This merits another conversation in which you can confront the seriousness of the problem. If that doesn't work, then encourage a parent or guardian to seek professional help. A mental health professional can coach a parent on how to get the teen into treatment.

3.3 MINISTRY TO FAMILIES WHO HAVE STRUGGLING TEENS

An eating disorder isn't just a teenager's problem—it's a family's problem. This type of disorder is very time intensive, complicated, draining, expensive, and frightening because it's a constant struggle that takes place in the shadow of a life-threatening problem. An eating disorder can easily become the focus of a family's existence. Schedules, priorities, values, behaviors, and relationships are all redefined in the light of this problem. The strain on the family can be great unless there is outside support. When there is no support, the toll on a family can be irreparable.

3.3A PERSONAL SUPPORT FOR PARENTS

Help parents talk to their teens. You may have to assist and support parents in their conversations with their teens just as you'd help teens talk to their parents. They may feel that your presence adds loving support and minimizes the potential for the meeting to escalate.

Resource parents. If parents believe their teens don't have a problem, suggest they read more about eating disorders and cue them into the signs and symptoms you've observed. Suggest that they at least take the teens to a qualified professional to make an assessment.

Listen to parents. They'll need to talk with someone about the struggles, sorrows, frustrations, and fears they're going through. Listening will encourage them to be patient with the process. Parents can often get caught in the trap of feeling guilt and blame. This can often distance the parents from their teens. Many times a parent can work through this with a trained therapist during family therapy, but a church can help by listening, loving, and reminding parents of the reconciling power of God to overcome Satan's accusations and our limited abilities. Shared faith in the goodness and restorative work of God becomes a powerful thing. We need to remind parents that we believe (even on their behalf) that God is healing even when they find it difficult to do that.

Connect parents with professional help. Many times parents won't know where to start once they detect that their teen has an eating disorder. If you've done some preventative work and already have a team of professionals that you can make referrals to, make that list available to the parents. In the event that you don't have resources in your area, coach parents to talk to their physician or contact national eating disorder organizations (like those listed in the "Resources" section of this book). I strongly recommend that parents look into a facility like Remuda Ranch. This Christian residential treatment center helps teens and families by taking a holistic and interdisciplinary treatment approach.

Support other siblings. Many times a parent's attention will be focused on the teen with the eating disorder. Younger siblings can often feel neglected or may lack the necessary understanding to weather the storm. The church can serve in a supportive way by taking an interest in those younger siblings, listening to their concerns, investing in them, and making sure their needs are met and their lives stay relatively normal. Parents will often welcome the help and support in this area. Sometimes a church can help by providing transportation and care when treatment interferes with the younger siblings' activities (in other words, taking them to sporting events, dance classes, and so on).

Help the family with mundane daily tasks. People from the church can help by occasionally providing meals for the family, running errands, grocery shopping, or providing house cleaning and lawn care, among other things.

Consider helping to cover the cost of treatment. Treatment is expensive, especially if residential treatment is necessary. The National Eating Disorder Association (NEDA) estimates that comprehensive, integrated treatment may cost more than $30,000 a month.[34] Some insurance providers don't cover the full interdisciplinary approach that's needed for effective results. So one way that a church community can help is by providing occasional financial assistance to a family. In addition, if a family member must leave a job temporarily in order to provide full-time care for a child with an eating disorder, they should look into the provision of the Family and Medical Leave Act (FMLA), which protects employees with family medical concerns that require their care.

3.3B WHAT IF A PARENT IS IN DENIAL?

Think about this scenario: You discover that a teen in your youth group is struggling with an eating disorder. After lovingly confronting the teen, he admits that these eating patterns and behaviors have been going on for about a year. You convince the teen he should tell his parents and seek immediate help. The teen agrees to do this, but a week after you discuss this matter, he still hasn't talked to his parents or taken any action.

When you ask the teen about this, you don't get a straight answer. You ask him if you can talk with his parents, and he reluctantly agrees. When you meet with the parents, they listen respectfully to your concerns but immediately make excuses for the teen and dismiss it as normal behavior. *What do you do? What can you do?*

Here are a few tips for helping parents who are in denial:

1. Always go with the teen to talk to the parents about something of this magnitude. Parental response is more gracious and thoughtful when an advocate is present. This will also give you insight into the family's feelings about this issue.

2. Provide materials for the parents so they can come to understand the severity of this disorder. They need to be educated about the signs, symptoms, and behaviors of a teen with an eating disorder.

3. Many parents (especially dads) will minimize the issue or believe they can quickly correct the problem by monitoring the teen's food intake. Emphasize the seriousness of this issue and that teens don't recover from this without the proper professional diagnosis and network of support.

4. Recommend that the teen be seen by a qualified health professional who can make an assessment. You can remind them that this is a very dangerous oversight if there is the possibility of a problem. The parents have nothing to lose by getting a professional to sign off, but if they don't—they could lose their teenager.

5. If the parents are still in denial, then you may have to take a more direct approach. Bring someone with you (another pastor from the church or someone else they respect) and lovingly confront the fact that you have an admission from their teen, as well as personal observations of a number of signs, symptoms, and behaviors that merit a professional assessment. Note: This should be done only if you have the kind of relationship with the parents that would allow you the privilege of being in their life so intimately.

6. Don't get into a battle with the parents or believe you need to convince them to do something. Make your suggestion and then monitor the teen whenever you're in contact. Realize that the confrontation may only drive a wedge between you and the parents, and they may not allow their child to come back to youth group afterward.

7. Realize that it may get worse before it gets better. If the teen lacks the necessary nutrition, he will start with milder physical

symptoms (like fainting and dizziness) that could lead him into the care of a physician.

8. In extreme cases where parents are unwilling to provide support or may be abusive, the teen can seek help without parental permission. A medical or mental health professional can make some judgments based on the well being of the teen apart from the parents' permission.

9. In cases where parents refuse to get help and the teen is resistant to seeking treatment, you can notify Child Protective Services (CPS) who will treat the incident as neglect. Chances are, an attending physician may also do this if the teen has been brought in for emergency treatment and the parents refuse treatment. But don't assume someone else will do it. If you're in doubt, call CPS, present the scenario, and seek their advice.

3.3C TIPS FOR PARENTS WHEN THEY ENGAGE THEIR TEENAGERS

Adolescence presents many challenges as teenagers explore pulling away from their parents and being more independent. An eating disorder just compounds these struggles and challenges. Often teenagers become rebellious and defiant when parents become aware of the eating disorder and step into the treatment process. And parents are often desperate for any assistance they can get. Here are some tips to help parents engage their struggling teens:

Avoid living vicariously through your teenager. Many parents have such strong desires to see their teens accepted by others as being beautiful, smart, or popular that they fail to praise and cultivate their teens' internal characteristics. These parents live vicariously through their children by making comments about their looks and weight. If a teen really needs to lose weight, make sure the conversations about the matter are centered on health, not looks. And make sure the teen's diet is monitored under the supervision of an adult, preferably a fitness trainer, nutritionist, or medical professional.

Don't tease, poke fun at, or criticize a teenager's weight. Don't allow siblings to attack the teen's looks, either.

Monitor your teen's online activities. Be aware that there are pro-anorexia and pro-bulimia Web sites that advocate eating disorders as an acceptable and admirable lifestyle alternative. Known as "Pro-Ana" or "Pro-Mia" sites, many have been banned by major search engines, but they are increasing in popularity and have become difficult to detect. Those teens who want to find them will do so. These sites are developed by people who struggle with eating disorders and body issues and have concluded that recovery is just a conspiracy to make them fat and ugly. They also perceive themselves to be similar to pro-smoking advocates who know there may be dangers to their behaviors, but they still protest any violation of their right to live the way they choose.

Continually encourage your teenager. Make a list of the top 10 things you love and appreciate about your teen and post it someplace where it's visible. Remind your teenager that the true quality of a person lies in these characteristics, not the package he or she comes in.

Examine your own values and attitudes toward food. Do you eat to feel better? Do you categorize foods as being good or bad? Are you constantly allowing your eating to get out of control and then dieting?

Talk about clothing choices. Teach your teens to wear clothing that makes them feel comfortable and not what emulates the size they think they should be. Model this yourself.

Encourage teens to be other-centered. An obsession with weight and looks is very self-focused. Help teens channel the energy and time they usually spend worrying about their looks into tutoring children, helping the elderly, serving in community social services like a food pantry or after-school programs, and a host of other things. Do this alongside teens to show them that giving is more important than being self-focused. Reaching out to others helps teenagers internalize Christ's command to love. This has a built-in fulfillment infusion that often transforms a teenager's perspective.

Monitor teenage athletes' workout routines. Many coaches' jobs are threatened by their teams' win-loss records. This underlying fear can compromise a coach's concern for the well-being of teenage athletes. A coach may push a bit harder or challenge students to drop weight so they can perform in a different weight class or improve their skills. Coaching can take on a negative, performance-driven style, rather than being positive and person-oriented. Parents need to be aware and be willing to confront an athletic department, school administration, or even the school board if athletes are being jeopardized.

Unfortunately, many parents don't want to interfere for fear the coach won't give their teens the opportunities or play times they deserve. Parents also fear their teens will face humiliation or ridicule as a result of their involvement, so they stay uninvolved until it's too late. Concerned parents should form a support committee that assists the team and coach in a positive way (many parents already do this), but they should also agree to monitor the coaching and training regimens to hold the athletic departments of their schools in an accountable profile.

If you're aware that your teen is struggling with one of the disorders described in this book, please note the following tips:

Seek professional help. Start by consulting your physician and then seek out a mental health professional who's trained or specializes in eating disorders. This complex problem will require a team of professionals. They can often be brought together through a clinic that specializes in eating and body image problems or under the direction of a qualified medical or mental health professional. And this should be done even if your teen refuses to seek help, in which case a qualified mental health professional can assist you in formulating an intervention.

Be loving and understanding. Affirm that you will always love your teen and that your love will never be altered or influenced by whatever struggle your teen is going through. Share that your desire is to understand and then show you mean it by educating yourself about the problem your teen is facing and the struggles involved. Ask your teen to help you understand the specific situation by giving him the authority to confront you whenever he feels like you aren't being understanding. This will help you see when your teen feels threatened or judged, even though that isn't your intent. It also gives the teen an appropriate sense of control. Try to see things from the teen's perspective. Teens with eating disorders don't usually make their decisions based on facts or logical reasoning; they rely on their emotions. So even if you describe and show a teen she isn't fat, she'll still believe she is because she *feels* fat. This doesn't mean you shouldn't use logic and reason; it just means you have to be loving, understanding, and patient.

Be patient. Realize that treatment may take a long time and be a slow process. One way you can show your patience is to help your teen feel secure in the process and in his relationship with you. Reassure him that you're in this for as long as it takes and your love for him won't be affected by it.

Keep a watchful eye on other destructive behaviors that your teen may develop. Sometimes teens will resort to binge alcohol drinking, drug use, or cutting as alternatives to eliminate their emotional pain.

Fight the eating disorder, not your teenager. Remember, this is a control issue and teens will often rebel against treatment or your involvement in their lives. Some therapists suggest that parents see the disorder as an evil intruder who's trying to destroy their children. Learn to recognize when the disorder is talking and influencing your teen's behavior. By personifying the eating disorder, teens can also begin to see and battle the eating disorder in a more tangible way.

Avoid oversimplifying the issue. Realize that telling affected teens to "just eat" or "stop throwing up" is asking them to do something that may be beyond their abilities. Often those responses are the result of a lack of understanding or parents' painful fear, frustration, and anger. When you get angry, remind teens that you aren't angry at them but at the situation.

Avoid being judgmental. As mentioned above, you may be angry at the situation and may even tell your teen that. But your teenager may still view your response as being judgmental. Make sure you talk this through and affirm that you know this is a horrible thing to have to struggle with. Realize that your teen is already experiencing self-condemnation and hatred over this issue. He or she may feel like a failure and totally worthless. Assure your teen that he or she is more valuable to you than anything else in your life.

Listen. The best way to show your love is to listen. Be available to let your teen talk things through but don't feel threatened if your teen prefers to talk with someone else. Realize that the normal adolescent response is to become an autonomous adult. However, parents still represent a lack of autonomy, so the typical teenage response is to break away from a parent's advice and help. Keep the doors open by listening whenever your teen wishes to talk with you and be encouraged if your teen is talking to someone who's in a position to help and support.

Declare your love for your teen. Teens with eating disorders need to be affirmed. Don't assume your teen knows you love him or her—declare it!

3.4 RAISING COMMUNITY AND CHURCH AWARENESS

Youth workers have done a very good job of raising the awareness of social concerns and injustice around the world. Many have championed issues of hunger and poverty, sex trafficking, illiteracy, water shortage, diseases from mosquitoes, AIDS, and more. But there are many other issues, such as eating disorders, that affect countless teenagers in the United States and around the world. Youth ministries can help provide awareness and support for these issues. More importantly, they need to take an active role in eradicating these deadly disorders that affect the lives of the global teenage population.

Here are some ways you can raise church and community awareness:

- National Eating Disorder Awareness Week (NEDAwareness Week) usually falls on the last week in February each year. This is a time when you can organize community events or bring the issue to the forefront of your church.
- Educate people regarding the prevalence, dangers, and warning signs of eating disorders. Start by requiring that all of your youth ministry workers be trained to recognize the warning signs and understand the dangers of eating disorders.
- Provide or sponsor speakers to go into the local high schools and address the issue in classes and assemblies. In conjunction with that, hold community-wide parent meetings to make parents aware of preventative and remedial measures they can take to make sure their teens don't fall victim to these disorders.
- Do a series on "Issues" or "Hot Topics" in a parent-teen class. Generate discussion on why the church needs to be more active regarding this issue. Show a documentary on eating disorders and then debrief in discussion groups.
- Open the church to host parent support groups.
- Have the youth group participate in fundraising efforts for eating disorders research. Or have your church begin a foundation that helps families offset the tremendous cost of treatment. Many families can't get treatment for their teenagers because the cost is so prohibitive (as much as $360,000 annually). Families are often ruined financially. Or if they come from low-income situations, they watch their teens die.

- Insert a short paragraph in your church newsletter or Web communications that explains the prevalence of eating disorders among teenagers and the destruction they cause.

Resources for Helping Teenagers Who Struggle With Eating Disorders

| Section 4 |

4.1A ONLINE RESOURCES

• Dove started its **Campaign for Real Beauty** back in 2004, and their TV commercials now reflect the natural beauty in girls and women. On their Web site, they provide workbooks, powerful video clips and interviews, and esteem-building exercises. Churches should support organizations like this that dare to run counter-culture and address the issues that affect so many teenage girls. http://www.dove.us/#/cfrb/

• Check out this amazing video entitled **"Evolution,"** put out by Dove's Campaign for Real Beauty. It shows that even supermodels are PhotoShopped to enhance their appearance, making the iconic perception of beauty more contrived and less attainable than ever. http://www.youtube.com/watch?v=iYhCn0jf46U

• The National Eating Disorders Association (NEDA) **provides free, downloadable Parent Toolkits** that help parents understand eating disorders and their treatment, provide assistance in mobilizing insurance payments, and much more. Find it at: http://www.nationaleatingdisorders.org/uploads/file/toolkits/NEDA-Toolkit-Parents_03-10-09.pdf.

• **Edreferral.com** (Eating Disorder Referral and Information Center) is the most comprehensive database of eating disorder professionals and treatment programs worldwide. Find them at www.edreferral.com.

4.1B NATIONAL AND INTERNATIONAL ORGANIZATIONS

• **The Renfrew Center Foundation**: Headquartered in Philadelphia, Pennsylvania, this isn't a Christian-based facility, but they do offer very effective research and treatment for girls who suffer from eating disorders. Their mission statement reads:

> The Renfrew Center Foundation is a tax-exempt, nonprofit organization advancing the education, prevention, research, and treatment of eating disorders. We advance our mission by:
> - Providing professional training and educational opportunities for mental health and medical professionals.
> - Creating awareness in the general public through the production of educational seminars and publications and participation in media-related activities.
> - Conducting research into the pathology and recovery patterns of people with eating disorders.
> - Educating policy makers to remove barriers to treatment.
> - Providing assistance for women and girls.

(http://www.renfrew.org/index.asp)

They also provide a downloadable reference guide for available printed resources at http://renfrewcenter.com/uploads/resources/1061827027_1.pdf.

• **National Eating Disorders Association (NEDA):** NEDA is the largest nonprofit eating disorder organization in North America.

Their mission statement reads: "NEDA supports individuals and families affected by eating disorders, and serves as a catalyst for prevention, cures and access to quality care." NEDA also has an Information and Referral Helpline at 1-800-931-2237. (http://www.nationaleatingdisorders.org)

• **Remuda Ranch:** This Christian treatment facility (with locations in Arizona and Virginia) ranks among one of the nation's best. I highly recommend them. I had the opportunity of working with Remuda Ranch when I was a young youth pastor in Arizona, and I've referred teens and their families to this program ever since. Their literature reads: "Remuda Ranch offers Christian inpatient and residential programs for individuals of all faiths suffering from eating or anxiety disorders. Each patient is treated by a multi-disciplinary team including a Psychiatric and a Primary Care Provider, Registered Dietitian, Masters Level therapist, Psychologist and Registered Nurse. The professional staff equips each patient with the right tools to live a healthy, productive life." For more information, call 1-800-445-1900 or visit www.remudaranch.com.

• **ReddStone** is Remuda Ranch's program for boys, ages 17 and under, who struggle with eating or anxiety disorders. It's worth distinguishing from Remuda Ranch's write-up because there are few programs designed just for males.

• **Canopy Cove.** This is another Christian treatment facility that provides comprehensive treatment for female and male adolescents and adults with eating disorders. Contact them at 800-236-7524 and check out their Web site at http://www.canopycove.com.

4.1C WRITTEN RESOURCES AND MEDIA

• *Behind the Broken Image* by Debra Cooper is a novel that traces the lives of three girls who are trapped in eating disorders. The book gives insight and hope to those who struggle with eating dysfunction and to those who are in the lives of a struggling teen. This book is a Remuda Ranch resource and is written from a Christian perspective.

• *Eating Disorders: A Handbook of Christian Treatment* by Edward J. Cumella, Marian C. Elerby, and A. David Wall. Another Remuda Ranch resource, the product description reads: "This book is one of the few comprehensive guides to eating disorders, including proper assessment and intervention, across the bio-psycho-social-spiritual continuum. Written for a broad range of healthcare and pastoral professionals, educators, and students, it offers state-of-the-art, scientifically valid knowledge of anorexia and bulimia nervosa, integrated with biblical Christianity. It can be the cornerstone of any eating disorders library."

• *Hunger for Freedom: My Spiritual Journey of Recovery* by Katie Gesto. This book speaks of Gesto's personal journey with an eating disorder. The great part about this resource is that it provides study questions, examples of recovery prayers, and Scripture encouragement in each chapter.

• *Thin Enough: My Spiritual Journey Through the Living Death of an Eating Disorder* by Sheryle Cruse. This book is written for adolescent girls. It takes the reader through a journey of learning to put faith and trust in God and fully understanding and becoming a daughter of God.

- *Diary of an Anorexic Girl* by Morgan Menzie. This story will help you understand the internal struggle of an eating disordered adolescent girl. It's great for youth workers to read and would also be a good tool for a struggling teen.

- *The Adonis Complex: The Secret Crisis of Male Body Obsession* by Harrison G. Pope Jr., Katharine A. Phillips, and Roberto Olivardia. This book explores the pressures that are put on teenage guys to strive for the perfect body. It uncovers practices that look relatively harmless but play into shaping the masculine identity of a young man.

- *Perfect Illusions: Eating Disorders and the Family* is a PBS documentary hosted by Lauren Hutton. It follows the lives of three girls and their struggles with eating disorders. It also reveals the roles and struggles their families faced during this terrible time. The documentary takes the viewer through the evolution, treatment, and recovery of someone with an eating disorder. For more information, check out the Web site, which also provides additional information and support on eating disorders, at http://www.pbs.org/perfectillusions.

- *Killing Us Softly*, *Still Killing Us Softly*, and *Killing Us Softly 3* are three powerful, award-winning documentaries by Jean Kilbourne that examine the effects of media and the messages it sends to young girls about their looks and identity. The Media Education Foundation provides a study guide and handouts to go along with these powerful films. You can find these videos at http://www.jeankilbourne.com/video.html.

• *Dying to be Thin* is a documentary produced by NOVA, which takes us into the research, causes, symptoms, and even history of eating disorders. This documentary is an exceptional resource because you can watch the entire documentary online at http://www.pbs.org/wgbh/nova/thin/program.html. It also has a very comprehensive Web site that provides a free teaching guide to accompany the video, current research, stories of those who've battled with eating disorders, insight into guys with eating disorders, and other helpful resources. You'll find this at http://www.pbs.org/wgbh/nova/thin.

• *Orthorexia: Obsessing Over Health Food* is a piece done by John Stossel for ABC's 20/20. The series gives insight regarding this deadly obsession, but Stossel's approach, although direct, shouldn't be followed when talking to a teen who's struggling. Watch the video at http://abcnews.go.com/Health/Stossel/story?id=5735592&page=1.

Notes

1. Jeffrey Zaslow, "Girls and Dieting, Then and Now," *Wall Street Journal*, September 2, 2009, http://online.wsj.com/article/SB10001424052970204731804574386822245731710.html.

2. Eating Disorder Clinic, "Eating Disorder Statistics," Eating Disorder Clinic, http://www.eatingdisorderclinic.org/eating-disorders-statistics.html.

3. South Carolina Department of Health, "Eating Disorder Statistics," South Carolina Department of Health, http://www.state.sc.us/dmh/anorexia/statistics.htm.

4. National Eating Disorders Association, "Statistics: Eating Disorders and Their Precursors," National Eating Disorders Association, http://www.nationaleatingdisorders.org/p.asp?WebPage_ID=286&Profile_ID=41138.

5. South Carolina Department of Health, "Eating Disorder Statistics," South Carolina Department of Health, http://www.state.sc.us/dmh/anorexia/statistics.htm.

6. P. F. Sullivan, "Mortality in Anorexia Nervosa," *American Journal of Psychiatry* 152, no. 7 (1995): 1073–1074.

7. National Eating Disorders Association, "Facts for Activists (or anyone!)," National Eating Disorders Association, http://www.nationaleatingdisorders.org/p.asp?WebPage_ID=286&Profile_ID=95634.

8. CDC Foundation, "Obesity: A Growing Epidemic," Centers for Disease Control and Prevention, http://www.cdcfoundation.org/healththreats/obesity.aspx, and Centers for Disease Control and Prevention, "Childhood Overweight and

Obesity," Centers for Disease Control and Prevention, http://www.cdc.gov/obesity/childhood/index.html.

9. Eating Disorder Clinic, "Eating Disorder Statistics," Eating Disorder Clinic, http://www.eatingdisorderclinic.org/eating-disorders-statistics.html.

10. Patrick Lyn, "Eating Disorders: A Review of the Literature with Emphasis on Medical Complications and Clinical Nutrition," *Alternative Medicine Review* (June 2002): 187–207.

11. M. Strober and C. Bulik, "Genetic Epidemiology of Eating Disorders" in *Eating Disorders and Obesity* 2nd ed., Christopher G. Fairburn and Kelly D. Brownell eds. (New York: The Guilford Press, 2002): 238–243.

12. Courtney E. Sanders, "The Physiology and Psychology of Bulimia," paper for Psychology 115 at Vanderbilt University, December 5, 1996, http://www.vanderbilt.edu/AnS/psychology/health_psychology/bulimia.htm.

13. Merry N. Miller, M.D. and A. Pumariega, M.D, "Eating Disorders: Culture and Eating Disorders," *Healthy Place: America's Mental Health Channel* (December 12, 2008), http://www.healthyplace.com/eating-disorders/main/eating-disorders-culture-and-eating-disorders/menu-id-58/.

14. Amelia J. Lake, Petra K. Staiger, and Huguette Glowinski. "Effects of Western Culture on Eating Attitudes and Body Image—Brief Article—Statistical Data Included," *Nutrition Research Newsletter* (Jan-April 2000). "Health Care Industry" page on BNET, FindArticles.com. (January 5, 2010), http://findarticles.com/p/articles/mi_m0887/is_2_19/ai_59969843/.

15. *Discover* Magazine, "Getting the Skinny on TV," Discover 20, no. 12 (Dec. 1999): 34–35, http://discovermagazine.com/1999/dec/newsofsciencemed1735.

16. Ginny Olson, *Teenage Girls: Exploring Issues Adolescent Girls Face and Strategies to Help Them* (Grand Rapids, MI: Zondervan/Youth Specialties, 2006), 55.

17. Catherine M. Shisslak, Marjorie Crago, and Linda S. Estes, "The Spectrum of Eating Disturbances," *International Journal of Eating Disorders* 18, no. 3 (1995): 209–219.

18. Female Athlete Triad Coalition, Mission Statement, *Female Athlete Triad Coalition*, http://www.femaleathletetriad.org/.

19. *Diagnostic and Statistical Manual of Mental Disorders*, 4th ed. Text Revision. (Washington, DC: American Psychiatric Association, 2000).

20. Dianne Neumark-Sztainer, *"I'm, Like, SO Fat!": Helping Your Teen Make Healthy Choices about Eating and Exercise in a Weight-Obsessed World* (New York: The Guilford Press, 2005), 5.

21. *Diagnostic and Statistical Manual of Mental Disorders*, 4th ed. Text Revision. (Washington, DC: American Psychiatric Association, 2000).

22. Ibid.

23. A&E, "Sonia & Julia," *Intervention*, episode 91, season 7.

24. Remuda Ranch, "Families Play a Role in the Development of Eating Disorders," *Remuda Ranch* (March 18, 2008), http://www.remudaranch.com/articles/families_play_role_in_eating_disorder_development/index.php.

25. Rudolph M. Bell, *Holy Anorexia* (Chicago: University of Chicago Press, 1985).

26. Ibid.

27. Ibid.

28. Mario Reda, "Anorexia and the Holiness of Saint Catherine of Siena," Graeme Newman trans., *Journal of Criminal Justice and Popular Culture* 8, no. 1 (2001): 37–47, http://www.albany.edu/scj/jcjpc/vol8is1/reda.html.

29. Remuda Ranch, "An Eating Disorder Reference for College Leaders," Remuda Ranch brochure, page 7, http://www.remudaranch.com/_pdf/College%20ED%20Brochure%200409.pdf.

30. AA Serenity, Recovery Prayers, http://www.aaserenity.com/recoveryprayers.html.

31. National Eating Disorders Association, "The Media, Body Image, and Eating Disorders," National Eating Disorders Association, http://www.nationaleatingdisorders.org/p.asp?WebPage_ID=286&Profile_ID=41166.

32. Linda Smolak, *National Eating Disorders Association/Next Door Neighbors Puppet Guide Book* (Seattle, WA: NEDA, 1996).

33. National Institute on Media and the Family, "Media's Effect on..." Fact Sheet, National Institute on Media and the Family, http://www.mediafamily.org/facts/facts_mediaeffect.shtml.

34. National Eating Disorders Association (NEDA), *The National Eating Disorders Association Parent Toolkit,* (Seattle, WA: NEDA, 2008), http://www.nationaleatingdisorders.org/uploads/file/toolkits/NEDA-Toolkit-Parents_03-10-09.pdf.

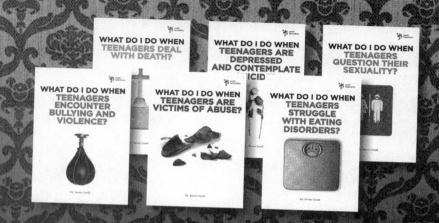

In this series of books designed for anyone connected to teenagers, Dr. Steven Gerali addresses six daunting and difficult situations that, when they do happen, often leave youth workers and parents feeling unprepared. With a background in adolescent counseling, Dr. Gerali provides valuable resources to help youth workers and parents through some of the most challenging situations they may face.

Each book defines the issue, explores how different theological perspectives can impact the situation, offers helpful, practical tips, along with credible resources to help the reader go deeper into the issues they're dealing with.

What Do I Do When Teenagers Encounter Bullying and Violence?

What Do I Do When Teenagers Deal With Death?

What Do I Do When Teenagers are Victims of Abuse?

What Do I Do When Teenagers are Depressed and Contemplate Suicide?

What Do I Do When Teenagers Struggle With Eating Disorders?

What Do I Do When Teenagers Question Their Sexuality?

youth
specialties

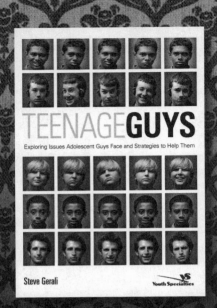

In *Teenage Guys*, author Steve Gerali breaks down the stages of development that adolescent guys go through, providing stories from his own experiences in ministry and counseling, as well as practical research findings to equip youth workers (both male and female)to more effectively minister to teenage guys. Each chapter includes advice from counselors and veteran youth workers, as well as discussion questions.

Teenage Guys
Exploring issues Adolescent Guys Face and Strategies to Help Them

Share Your Thoughts

With the Author: Your comments will be forwarded to the author when you send them to *zauthor@zondervan.com.*

With Zondervan: Submit your review of this book by writing to *zreview@zondervan.com.*

Free Online Resources at
www.zondervan.com

Zondervan AuthorTracker: Be notified whenever your favorite authors publish new books, go on tour, or post an update about what's happening in their lives at www.zondervan.com/authortracker.

Daily Bible Verses and Devotions: Enrich your life with daily Bible verses or devotions that help you start every morning focused on God. Visit www.zondervan.com/newsletters.

Free Email Publications: Sign up for newsletters on Christian living, academic resources, church ministry, fiction, children's resources, and more. Visit www.zondervan.com/newsletters.

Zondervan Bible Search: Find and compare Bible passages in a variety of translations at www.zondervanbiblesearch.com.

Other Benefits: Register yourself to receive online benefits like coupons and special offers, or to participate in research.